The Miraculous Image
of the
Madonna of Rimini

DOLOROSA PRESS
Bristol, MMXII

THE MIRACULOUS IMAGE
OF THE MADONNA OF RIMINI

Copyright © 2012 by Paul M. Kimball
All rights reserved.

No part of this book may be reproduced or transmitted in any form or by any means, electronic or mechanical, including information and retrieval systems, without permission in writing from the copyright holder, except by a reviewer who may quote brief passages in a review.

ISBN: 978-0-9883723-0-6

Additional copies available from Dolorosa Press at *http://www.dolorosapress.com/*

PREFACE

On July twenty-seventh, eighteen hundred and fifty, the following account of the miracle of Our Lady of Mercy in Rimini was published in three Catholic periodicals: *The Tablet, The Catholic of Genoa,* and *The Lamp.* The author of this account had been two days "contemplating the blessed image" and "collecting circumstantial details" from all classes of persons.

"Yesterday, I saw the Madonna, whose eyes are ordinarily turned towards Heaven, bend them towards the pious multitude, when the faithful from five different parishes were attending the celebration of the Mass. I saw the eyes in the painting of Our Lady of Mercy move downwards, and that ceasing to direct themselves to the vault of the Church, they fixed themselves perpendicularly on the vault situated opposite the altar. The physiognomy, habitually mournful, had taken during this Mass an expression of joy, as if she wished to signify that she accepted the homage of this multitude. Yesterday I was able to approach the altar so as to touch it, then again I was a witness of the movement of the eyes.

"There is not the means, as many imagine, of any mechanical contrivance, such as a statue with springs; the pupils which in their ordinary state are altogether visible raise themselves so high that at some moments they seem to disappear, and the eye appears all white. One might imagine that it is an effect of lassitude, for they say that after long and sustained attention, the object appears to the fatigued eye to move and change. But what forbids all doubt is that at the very moment when my eyes saw the prodigy, all round me saw it simultaneously.

"In the evening I wished to examine the picture closely and having obtained permission of the Reverend Missionary Fathers, I remained until the closing of the Church, and was then able to touch the picture. During nearly the hour in which twelve other persons and I spent in observing it, we no longer perceived any movement.

"In the presence of a multitude of people, the triers (appointed for legal and solemn visitation) made the most minute investigation, at the close of which, they declared that there was neither artifice nor secret contrivance, and that the occurrence could not have been produced by the hand of man. These results are notorious. On the evening of the eighteenth, as several priests and seculars related to me, the Marquis of Pepoli of Bologna not only saw the prodigy with his eyes, but saw it in a manner so sensible that his emotion made him faint away. On coming to himself, he took his watch from his neck, and suspended it on the picture, where I saw it yesterday. [*Here are names and facts, editor.*] It is true, that up to the present time, the miraculous cures have not been as numerous as some reports have stated. But may the most skeptical be convinced by the letter of the Bishop of Rimini to the editors of the *Armonia*, in answer to a request for 'official information':

> Rimini, June 24, 1850. 'The public testimony of people of every condition, etc., renders worthy of all belief, the movement of the eyes of our holy picture of Mary, Mother of Mercy, a miracle which has not ceased for fifty days up to the present hour. This extraordinary event is verified by a judicial enquiry, pursued in my Palace; and the documents and proofs of the fact will be published in due time.'"

In response to this published account, the minister of Highbury Chapel in Birmingham, Reverend Brewin Grant, B.A., published a scathing attack upon this account in a discourse on October twenty-seventh, eighteen hundred and fifty, and later published in a booklet entitled: *Rimini and Oxford: or, The Miraculous Picture of Mary, and a Divine Portrait of the Church. Dedicated without permission to Pius IX*. In it can be found impious words bemoaning devotion to the Blessed Mother of God such as the following: "But the Pope's letter on this subject [Papal Brief of Pope Pius the Ninth authorizing the coronation of the image of the miraculous image of Our Lady of Mercy in Rimini dated July twenty-fifth, eighteen hundred and fifty], is both a proof of how willingly he joins in such artifices, and of how fully the Romish Church is involved in idolatry. The absurdity and pestiferous superstition to which this Papal letter gives sanction, though not more ridiculous is more blasphemous than the tale of the Winking Picture." Yet this miracle was verified by a diocesan commission which studied the matter and on January eleventh, eighteen hundred and fifty-one, the Bishop of Rimini issued a decree stating: "that the truth of the marvelous movement of the pupils in the holy image of the Blessed Virgin Mary, under the title of the Mother of Mercy has been and remains proven."

The fury of heretics and hence of hell should be a signal to devout Catholic readers of the importance of this miracle. For it substantiates by empirical evidence the claims of God's Church to be the true Church founded by Jesus Christ, and that His Most Holy Mother is worthy of a very special honor not given even to any other saint, which the theologians call *hyperdulia*.

The historical context of this miracle is also significant. This verified and proven miracle took place twenty years before the Masonic takeover of the Papal States wherein the miracle took place. The miracle was likely to bolster up the faith of Catholics living there before the deluge of anti-Catholic and secular propaganda would threaten their regions of Italy, hitherto well-guarded though the paternal vigilance of the popes against the erroneous principles of the bloody French Revolution, which elsewhere had already spread throughout Europe and most of the world.

The particular occasion that prompted the editor of this booklet to publish this account, was his visit to Rimini at the beginning of this year. There he met the pastor at the Church of Saint Clare, namely a Missionary of the Most Precious Blood, who told him the story of the miracle of Our Lady of Mercy which took place in eighteen hundred and fifty. The editor then told the Missionary about a similar miracle in Quito, Ecuador, where the eyes in the picture of the Sorrowful Mother of the school of Saint Gabriel first moved during fifteen minutes in front of forty students, and then repeated during a *Triduum* in honor of the image, when the newly appointed Archbishop himself saw the miracle. The Missionary replied, "Three days! Here the miracle lasted nine months!" He also mentioned that Saint John Bosco attended the twenty-fifth anniversary Mass in the Church of Saint Clare.

May this booklet then help to make known to the English-speaking world this little-known yet striking miracle of Our Lady of Mercy in Rimini, for her honor and for the sustaining of the faith of

Catholics during this time of world-wide apostasy; "For it is good to hide the secret of a king: but honorable to reveal and confess the works of God" (Tobias 12, 7).

Finally, may the reader offer a prayer for the capable translator who generously undertook the task of making this text available to English readers. His name is not given here because the translation from the Italian was written by a French religious whose name is not recorded and this English translation pays deference to the same convention.

Bristol, England, September 18, 2012,
Feast of Saint Joseph Cupertino.

REVEREND PAUL M. KIMBALL,
Priestly Fraternity of Saint Pius X

Approved by the Archdiocese of Malines

Having examined the booklet entitled
*The marvelous movement of the eyes
of the sacred image of Mary Most Holy
under the title of Mother of Mercy,*
We authorize its printing.

Malines, January 7, 1853

P. CORTEN, Vicar General

MOTHER OF MERCY

Venerated in the Church of Saint Clare in Rimini. In May of 1850,
the eyes of image moved miraculously in the sight of many witnesses.

The Miraculous Image of the Madonna of Rimini

Extract from the official Canonical Process
carried out by the Diocesan Ecclesiastical Authority.

Translated from the French edition of the original Italian.

TABLE OF CONTENTS

—

PREFACE iii

TRANSLATOR'S NOTE 13

INTRODUCTION 15

CH. I   The image's origins and description. Its donation to the Church of Saint Clare. 16

CH. II   The faithful's devotion to the holy image. The beginning of the miraculous events. The gathering of the faithful. The holy image's Relocation to the high altar. The people's emotion and ending of blasphemies. 18

CH. III   The removal of the glass from the holy image. The Bishop of Rimini's arrival and pronouncement. Spiritual exercises and the image's relocation to the Church of Saint Augustine. 21

CH. IV   The spiritual exercises' beneficial effects. Postponement of the holy image's return to Saint Clare's. New procession, etc. 24

CH. V   The commencement of the Judicial Process and subsequent miracle. The given reasons for this. . 25

CH. VI   Sworn statements from witnesses of the marvel on May eleventh and twelfth in the small chapel of Saint Clare's. 31

CH. VII   Sworn statements from witnesses of the miracle from May twelfth through the eighteenth at high altar of Saint Clare's, both before and after the holy image's glass removal. 34

CH. VIII	Sworn statements from witnesses of the miracle at Saint Augustine's.	39
CH. IX	Sworn statements from simultaneous witnesses of the miracle, as well as of verbal or signal intercommunicators of its happening.	43
CH. X	Sworn statements from witnesses of the miracle: a) according to the image's different positions and levels of light; b) in the public square; c) on the very mensa of the altar.	46
CH. XI	The indubitable certainty of the miracle achieved by a seven-person experiment.	51
CH. XII	Sworn statements from witnesses of changes in the miraculous image: the face's color, tears from the eyes, and lip movement.	55
CH. XIII	Graces accorded to the faithful through the intercession of the Blessed Virgin.	58
CH. XIV	Conviction of the truth and certainty of the miracles. The growth of devotion to the Blessed Virgin. Visits to the holy image. Its solemn coronation. .	61
CH. XV	Offerings made to the made to the Most Holy Virgin.	66
CH. XVI	Conclusion and Decree of the Bishop concerning the miracle.	69
PRAYER TO OUR LADY		**74**
IMAGE GALLERY		**75**

TRANSLATOR'S NOTE[1]

The miracle of Rimini has had an immense impact, and it is impossible to forget the stir it caused throughout the world.

The Bishop of Rimini has just authorized the publication of an authentic account of the event. This account has, as its crowning feature and by way of conclusion, the Episcopal decree which recognizes and confirms the truth of the miracle.

It has seemed to us that a translation of this booklet will not be without value and will bring pleasure to the numerous people who have been interested in the time and circumstances which it relates.

Those who have believed will find in this work an ample confirmation of their faith.

Those who have doubted will be able to shed light on their difficulties, and, if they are in good faith, we hope that they will not resist the evidence or the impact of the witness testimonies which have been collected in this simple but convincing exposition.

As for those who have blasphemed the love of Mary, we know what impression will be made on them by the brilliance of the truth. We wish that it will be a favorable impression and that they will abjure their foolish mocking and their disgusting blasphemies. We wish this most fervently, and will ask it of the holy Virgin.

We have tried to preserve the character and simplicity of the account, and have translated as literally as possible; perhaps too literally. We have in particular sought to be faithful: so that we cannot be reproached for lacking an elegance which we have not sought to display. Whatever the faults of style, we like to persuade ourselves that the devotees of Mary will not read without edification this account of one of the greatest displays of her power and her love of which this century has been the witness.

---

1. This note is taken from the French edition, which is the source of this English translation.

INTRODUCTION

Founded by Jesus Christ, and sealed by His precious Blood on Calvary, the Catholic Church offers for our inspection an assembly of marvels and an infinite series of wonders. Across the centuries, where struggles seem to multiply against her; across a thousand heresies, a thousand schisms and a thousand terrible wars which have assailed her to the point where she has seemed beaten; chased from the heart of men and banished from the whole world; the Church has always arisen more beautiful, and has won the most magnificent triumphs over her enemies and over her persecutors. For God, who has promised that she will exist until the consummation of the world, watches like a faithful guardian and like an invincible defender over His well-beloved spouse; also, just as in times of calm, He opens up before her, with infinite wisdom and admirable art, a road strewn with flowers, and He plaits her hair with triumphal crowns; so also, in the middle of the most terrible and frightening persecutions He embellishes her with splendid palms and trophies. Every man who works through history and applies himself to the study of her annals cannot underestimate this truth, and it is impossible for him not to recognize the care taken by Divine Providence to conserve and exalt her. From the crib in Bethlehem to the cross on Calvary; from Calvary to the Apostles; from the Apostles to the martyrs; from the martyrs to the Doctors; from the Doctors to the Confessors, it is the most solemn and most magnificent panegyric. What lies, perfidiousness, violence, hypocritical regrets, scorn, calumnies, and what axes have been ranged against her! But God, in His infinite mercy and goodness, one way or another, has always come to her aid; so as to confound and disarm the proud wisdom and deceitful malice of the unbelievers; in order to bring back to the way of goodness the victim of error; to reaffirm the faithful in the Faith, He has worked ineffable wonders and caused marvelous events. The Gospel, the Acts of the Apostles, the writings of the holy Fathers, the fasts of the Martyrs and Confessors show infinite examples of this, and every man who has retained the light of intelligence cannot ever mistake them.

That is why, when we consider the terrible war that, in our own days, has been openly declared against the Christian religion and the tireless efforts of the northern heretics to overthrow the foundations of the Catholic Church; when we remember the appalling falling away of so many children from this immortal and immaculate bride of Jesus Christ, in the middle of such a shamelessness of incredulity, in the middle of such an overflowing of criminal and sacrilegious actions, we believe that we are not departing from truth by affirming that God has desired, in His impenetrable decrees and by means of an image of His Sacred Mother, to cause, today, in Rimini, a new marvel for the salvation of men and the exaltation of the Catholic Church.

Let us also recognize that there is great benefit, for the glory of truth, for the consolation of the faithful and for the instruction of those who have become lost, in making known to the public this marvelous event which has happened before our eyes and within our walls, so that the renowned event—which has spread, not only in Italy, but throughout all of Europe and even beyond, and of which our account is written in all simplicity—will cause truth and indestructible authenticity to be revealed.

CHAPTER I

The image's origins and description.
Its donation to the Church of Saint Clare.

Distinguished not as much by his birth as by the spotless brilliance of religion and by the holiness of his life which he preserved until his death; such was Giuseppe Soleri Brancaleoni, noble patrician of Rimini. From his earliest years he applied himself with great care to painting and he studied under excellent masters. His progress was rapid, but in order to acquire perfection in his art, he went to Rome, the true mistress of the fine arts. He had not been long in that city when he was afflicted by a slow but dangerous illness and the doctors could find no better remedy than to persuade him to return to his home state. It cost him dearly to follow their advice, so strong was his love for painting; nevertheless, he obeyed, and once somewhat recovered from his infirmity, consecrated himself completely to his art. With the intention, by his example and advice, of helping young people who, like him, were devoted to art, he opened a studio in his own house. His brush produced many works, and it is still possible to find many of them in the town.

It is not our place to assess the quality of this work, and even if it were, we would willingly pass over the responsibility; for the purposes we have set ourselves it would be a pointless thing to do. We would just say that it is wonderful praise and a great happiness for a pious artist to have been the creator of the holy image of the Virgin Mary, known by the title of *Mother of Mercy*, which, in our time, has here shown movement of its eyes. In all probability it was in seventeen hundred and ninety-six or around that year when the image was painted in oils, being sixty centimeters in height and seventy-two centimeters in width. The holy virgin is represented in half-figure with an elegant and well-chosen expression; she holds her hand lightly placed on her bosom; her head is lightly resting on her right shoulder; her eyes are raised to Heaven. Her face is rendered with tints so delicate that when one contemplates it, one starts to love, and is seized with the thought that Mary, in interceding for mankind, is employing all her love, all her prayers, all the intensity of her look, which is lost in God. One might say that she is rejoicing in being heard, and that she is sharing her joy with her servants; one might believe that in the rapture of her heavenly thoughts she is allowing to slip spontaneously from her lips the words of the canticle:

> *My soul doth magnify the Lord,*
> *And my spirit hath rejoiced*
> *in God my Savior,*
> *Because He hath regarded*
> *the humility of His handmaid:*
> *For behold, from henceforth,*
> *all generations shall call me blessed,*
> *Because He that is mighty*
> *hath done great things to me.*

A special devotion and such a sweet memory of the pious creator determined the Brancaleoni family to take great care of this precious picture and, from a pious jealousy, to keep it out of sight in the family home. But several people of piety who were friends of the family, having often had the chance to admire it, were compelled both by their own desire and by that of a great number of others to make known to all their fellow citizens that this was a fine and pleasing work, and to cause it to be exposed in a church for the veneration of the public, and so with the most fervent prayers they asked for this favor. God permitted that the pious family should agree with kindness to this request, and in eighteen hundred and ten, with the most praiseworthy generosity, by means of a deed of gift, they gave it to the neighboring Church of Saint Clare.[2] This church had previously belonged to a monastery of nuns, and was now in the possession of the Missionaries of the Most Precious Blood of Our Lord Jesus Christ, whose ardent and tireless zeal for the welfare of souls cannot be praised highly enough.

CHAPTER II

The faithful's devotion to the holy image. The beginning of the miraculous events.
The gathering of the faithful. The holy image's relocation to the high altar.
The people's emotion and ending of blasphemies.

Exposed, as we have said, to the veneration of the public in the Church of Saint Clare, the holy image immediately became the object of piety and the bustling attention of the faithful. The fervor of devotion experienced for it inspired the formation of a pious society in its honor, and the celebration of festivals in its praise, in which the greatest splendors were modesty and reverence. This throng and this devotion were never interrupted, and no one entered the small Church of Saint Clare without making a visit to the holy Virgin and saying a prayer to her before leaving. We could perhaps have omitted these details, but we recall them with pleasure, especially because they are true and also because it seems to us that they weigh importantly on the question which concerns us. Whatever the case may be, if, over so many years that the holy image was venerated and admired

---

2. *Santuario Madonna della Misericordia (S. Chiara)*, via S. Chiara, 28 — 47921 Rimini.

by such a large number of the faithful, no one ever mentioned any miraculous movement, it seems to us reasonable to conclude with justification that what we have seen happening in our days is no illusion, but an unchallengeable truth. We are now going to speak about the miracle, and hope, to the glory of the Most Holy Virgin, to produce some proofs of nature, so as to leave no possible doubt as to its authenticity.

It was on May eleventh, eighteen hundred and fifty, a day and month that seem to us noteworthy, it being a Saturday in the month of May, a month and day both consecrated to the Most Holy Virgin. Lady Anna Bugli, countess Baldini, accompanied by her adoptive daughter, Anna Achilli, and Francesca Megani were passing by chance in front of the Church of Saint Clare around one-thirty in the afternoon. She was not accustomed to attending this church, but on that day God permitted her to feel compelled by some interior sense to enter. So, she went inside with the two girls and made for the side chapel where the holy image was placed on a small altar, and she began to pray in front of it. But what a surprise she had when, fixing her view on this heavenly face, she saw (a spectacle worthy of heaven and the angels) its holy pupils gently moving and rising to the point where they disappeared completely under the eyelids. She could not doubt the marvel, but at the same time she did not dare to believe her own eyes; that is why she called to the two young girls who were kneeling a little further away, and she made them share in the marvel, asking them to examine carefully if they were also able to see what she had seen. The young girls submitted with good heart, and, so as to see better, they went onto the step of the altar, getting so close to the picture that they could almost touch it if they stretched out their arms, and they stayed there with attention, fixing their eyes on those of the Virgin. They did not need to wait long; what the countess had seen a little earlier was granted to both the countess and to them to see again. Both of them, at the same time and in the clearest and most incontrovertible way, perceived the movement, and in the short space of the half hour that they stayed in the chapel, it was granted to them to see several further occurrences. Convinced of the truth of the marvel, and moved by tenderness, but suffering from a mixture of joy and holy fervor, they moved away and left the church.

Such was the beginning of the wonder; in this way it had as its first witnesses three people worthy of complete trust. The next day, Sunday, May twelfth, the two young girls, whom the countess had advised, as a precaution, not to tell anyone in the world what they had seen, came back Saint Clare's alone (the countess being unwell) and they again entered the chapel of the wonderful Virgin. There they found a woman called Elena Scaramucci; another woman called Anna Mariani and Mistress Eleanora Borglioni (née Marchesa Buonadrata) arrived a little later. God, wishing perhaps, that the marvel should have a greater number of witnesses, renewed it, and in such a way that all these people could see it very clearly and markedly. On seeing this miracle, they were seized by a great astonishment, and they judged it appropriate to inform the Missionary Fathers. So, they went to look for one of these religious, and having found him they gave him an account of the whole matter. From their manner and the certainty of their words; from their features, their gestures, their emotion and the tears which escaped from their eyes it was easy for the religious priest to see that there was within their account nothing less than a real wonder. He immediately went to the chapel, and after looking attentively at the eyes of the Virgin, he declared that he could not see anything. However, he thought it wise to recommend that the young girls go and examine another image of the Virgin which was in the church, and to consider carefully whether they could see any movement of the eyes in this other image. These good girls went and looked attentively, but saw nothing; and accordingly they came back to the priest and confirmed that they had not seen any movement. So, pulling back the curtain of the window that opened onto the chapel, the religious knelt down in front of the Virgin and started to recite the litanies. He had hardly started the recitation of this prayer when the witnesses assisting him saw the marvel once again; and at the very instant that they started to see it, they noticed in him a certain hesitation and trembling in his whole person, and they realized that he had become convinced.

In the afternoon, news of the marvel had spread out all over the town and among all classes of the population, from the palaces of the rich to the most miserable habitations of the destitute. People began to tell one another; they asked questions; they answered; they were amazed; they marveled; they shed tears of tenderness, and everyone ran to the holy image of the Mother of Mercy. In no time the chapel of the holy Virgin and the church were filled with a pious multitude and the neighboring roads were full of people. However, the ecclesiastical court had been informed of the wonder, and of the immense gathering of population, and so of his own accord the illustrious and reverend Monsignor Michele Brioli, Provost of the illustrious Chapter and General Provincial, took himself to the Church of Saint Clare. With great difficulty he was able to open up a passage through the tightly-packed crowd, and he went up to the sacred image, he venerated it devoutly, took it into his hands and transported it to the high altar, onto which he placed it. Upon seeing this, the faithful, in the midst of their moans and tears were heard to cry out the most touching cries of "Long live Jesus, long live Mary!" along with the most resounding exclamations of "No more sins! No more blasphemies!"—cries and exclamations from the heart which were inspired in some of them by the strength of their faith and their devotion to Mary; in others by the evidence of the marvel which was taking place before their eyes. Oh! How admirable is the Lord, and how merciful! How many were those who, having gone astray, came back at this moment to the friendship of God and the peace of their consciences! How blasphemy stopped at that moment, mute and shameful: that thing which, only days before, had excited horror in the hearts of the faithful and had even made the dumb walls themselves quiver!

CHAPTER III

The removal of the glass from the holy image.
The Bishop of Rimini's arrival and pronouncement.
Spiritual exercises and the image's relocation to the Church of Augustine.

Just as on the two days of which we have just spoken, so during the following days the marvel continued, and became even more perceptible and frequent. All day long and for a large part of the night the church was full, and it was not only the inhabitants of Rimini who were there with ever-growing eagerness, but also a crowd of folk from the countryside and the neighboring villages.

As time went by, the number of eyewitnesses to the marvel grew and the rumor spread more and more; and although fame is accustomed to exaggerating everything, this was one matter which it was unable to exalt adequately or to give sufficient dignity. But even the clearest and most evident truths often find malevolent opponents rather than severe critics; and it is good that this should be so, because, by denigrating the worth which surrounds them they serve to raise the splendor of truth and to assure it of its triumph. Some people, whether driven by habit or by the desire to acquire for themselves the renown of being prudent men and of sensible judgment, or for some other reason (which it is not valuable to speculate on here) started at first to deny the existence or the possibility of the marvelous event; later, convinced by the authority of upright and sensible men who had seen the miracle with their own eyes, they went around everywhere repeating that all of this was nothing but an illusion and a play of light produced by the glass in front of the image of the Virgin. As soon as the priest had become aware of these suggestions, and in order to ensure that the reality of this marvel might shine out in all purity and certainty, and so that no basis for doubt or objection might remain, he had the wise idea of going up to the venerated image and taking off the glass (which was clear and clean) and of showing the completely clear cover to the great crowd. Having explained the reason for his actions, he put the image back in its place. On seeing this and hearing his words, the assembled crowd let out a great roar of indignation and its praises of Mary became ever more animated and affectionate. But did the removal of the glass cause the miracle to cease? Not at all: on the contrary, it continued with ever greater splendor and clarity, as we will make clear in due course.

 Things were at this stage when His Excellency, the Reverend Monsignor Salvatore Leziroti, our most vigilant and wise Bishop, who was at that time out in his diocese on a pastoral visit, was informed of the marvelous wonder, and he immediately interrupted his visit and came back without delay to his Episcopal city. What a consolation it was for all classes of citizen, at such a solemn moment, to see the arrival of their chief pastor; it hardly needs to be said! They waited for him, the wisdom of his advice and the consolation of his spiritual succor. The public's expectation was soon satisfied by a most salutary response, and in an announcement on May fifteenth, after mentioning the miraculous event, the mercies of the Lord and the need for the reform of morals, he declared that everything was in place for a ten-day course of extraordinary spiritual exercises to be given by wise and truly apostolic men. The Church of Saint Clare was too small for such a preaching mission, so he most wisely decided that the exercises should take place in the huge Church of Saint John the Evangelist, called Saint Augustine's, and that the amazing image of the wonderful Mother of God should be taken there for the duration of the mission. May eighteenth was the day fixed for the beginning of the holy exercises and for the solemn translation of the most Holy Virgin. As soon as dawn broke on the happy day, the faithful rushed from everywhere, in crowds so large that it was not possible to recall such numbers (not even when the Blessed Pius the Seventh returned from his country of exile, surrounded by the joy of the people and showing a new triumph of the Church by his presence as he passed by Rimini and went up to his City of Rome to sit again on the cornerstone which, despite the attacks of the devil, remains steadfast until the end of the world). In the center of this large crowd, and through the streets decorated as on feast days, the Bishop, the chapter, the judges, the college of priests and all the city worthies went in procession from the cathedral to the Church of Saint Clare. There they took up the holy image, and the procession moved slowly towards Saint Augustine's to the ringing of bells; and even today one can scarcely remember the holy ceremony without being moved to tears! Oh what a beautiful spectacle it was, to see a countless number of people having no thought but of Mary, falling to their knees before her, turning their looks full of love towards her, shedding tears of tenderness, whilst the canticles and sacred hymns that were sung with the sweetest of melodies by the choirs of young servers filled the soul with an ineffable sweetness, and the holy Virgin herself filled them all with heavenly emotions that they had not known before then. Oh! How great were the inspirations of religion! Unlucky was he who was not able to appreciate them!

Once the holy image had arrived at the Church of Saint Augustine and had blessed the people, it was placed on the altar that had been prepared to receive it, and the spiritual devotions began.

CHAPTER IV

The spiritual exercises' beneficial effects.
Postponement of the holy image's return to Saint Clare's. New procession, etc.

The apostolic works of men who were tireless in their fervor to obtain, in every possible way, the spiritual good of souls, produced consoling and wonderful results, and the hand of God was shown to be prodigious in the supernatural favors that were achieved. There were not enough priests to hear the confessions, and everywhere to be wondered at, were the clearest signs of the recovery of faith, of gratitude, of piety, of the eradication and death of sin; in a word, of the most beautiful virtues and the holiest and most sincere resolutions. And, indeed, if in all apostolic works of this kind it is common to bring in a great harvest of good and to win for God a great number of souls, what superabundance of fruits is it not possible to gain, and what a huge number of souls cannot be conquered for heaven with the help of the extraordinary assistance of the miraculous image? What heart, however hard or unfeeling, could remain indifferent and not reduced to tears of contrition on seeing the holy pupils of the Mother of Mercy move in the presence of everyone present?

However, the end of the spiritual exercises was approaching and the day on which (according to what had been determined) it was necessary to return the holy image to the church from which it had been taken. In view, however, of the increasing numbers of foreign visitors of every rank and station, distinguished by nobility of birth or by the elevation of their station, who were arriving from all parts of Italy and other regions of Europe; in view as well of the numerous and devout processions, not only from the diocese of Rimini but also from neighboring dioceses, that were starting to take place to visit the powerful Mother of God; the ecclesiastical authority hesitated about ordering the return of the image for the good reason that the Church of Saint Clare was not large enough to receive such an immense number of the faithful. Such a thought was in the mind of the wise magistrature who, after mature deliberation, made representation to the Bishop, asking him to take into account the well-being of the faithful and to consider the various places where the Most Holy Virgin might be venerated. They begged him, if he wished to avoid confusion and many other inconveniences, to suspend the return of the miraculous image to its church, and to leave it at Saint Augustine's as long as was necessary, until an alternative could be found. His Excellency, convinced by the wisdom of the suggestion, was favorably disposed to their petition, and ordered the Virgin to remain at Saint Augustine's until further order might be given. But, as it had been promised that a further procession would take place on the occasion of the return of the image, the Bishop did not wish to cancel it, so he ordered the holy image to be carried in procession through the main streets of the city and brought back to Saint Augustine's. This was duly done, and on May twenty-eighth, there took place this fresh solemnity, which filled Rimini with a new joy. It was in all respects like the first, and inspired the same universal emotion; it received an even greater splendor because of the presence of a number of great and worthy people who came along with the magistrature of the city and the distinguished governor. The Bishops of Faenza and Pesaro were present along with members of the clergy, the Council deputation, and the brotherhoods of Pesaro which, in a fine example of devotion, had come to take part in the ceremony and to venerate the most powerful Mother of Mercy, bringing her in homage not only very rich presents, but also (more importantly) offerings to her of the hearts of these pious and honorable citizens.

All that we have recounted so far is not unconnected to our topic, because it is easy to draw from it much important evidence that validates the truth of the miracle. We could speak of many things of the same kind; but we believe that for the time being it is better to interrupt this part of the story and reserve it for another place, and that it is preferable to speak more specifically about the miracle, so as to expose it and consequently demonstrate the truth of it. That is what we are going to do for the consolation of the faithful, and so as to convince the most rebellious spirits.

CHAPTER V

The commencement of the Judicial Process and subsequent miracle.
The given reasons for this.

From the moment that the Bishop interrupted his diocesan visit and returned to the episcopal city, he remained convinced of the truth of the wonderful marvel, on the evidence of honest and sensible men of integrity. But nevertheless, although he detected the hand of God, and he was persuaded as to the reality of what had been happening up to that time (and was continuing to happen on a daily basis); in order that he might provide greater certainty in these days of defiance and disbelief, and so as to provide more evidence of the wonderful working of the infinite Providence of God; under decree of May fifteenth, by means of a motion in court of the procurator fiscal of the Court, Carlo Gaspard Venturini, he ordered the setting up of an accurate and formal legal process: a very wise decision, the wisdom of which was proved, not only by the great success which it enjoyed, but even more so by the order which later resulted from His Holiness Pope Pius the Ninth, still happily reigning, by letter of the Sacred Congregation of Bishops and Regulars, dated May eighteenth, eighteen hundred and fifty.

Before coming to the demonstration of the proofs which establish the certainty of the miracle, perhaps it might not be out of place to say something about the possibility of miracles. But since this question has been dealt with by a large number of apologists of the Catholic faith and has been victoriously demonstrated, so that no doubt can possibly remain, and since, moreover, one only has to reflect on the infinite omnipotence of God, it is impossible not to recognize in such omnipotence the most profound of reasons and not become firmly convinced. As a result, we have decided to pass over this point in silence. In the present case, the possibility of the marvelous event is no longer in question; the event took place, and that is why in our opinion we only need to research one thing: to decide whether the event is truly miraculous, and then whether the proofs on which it rests have an unassailable power and truth. The first point will be established if we can demonstrate that the movement of the eyes of the holy image of the blessed Mother of Mercy is contrary to the constant laws of nature; that it could not have been produced by any natural cause; and that, as a result, it can only be attributed to the supreme Author and Judge of nature herself. The second point will be proven if we can establish that the movement has been seen and attested by acceptable witnesses and confirmed by their canonical depositions and solemn oaths. We will speak very briefly of the first point, because we will have a great deal to say about the second, which is principal focus of our account.

Let us begin by proving that the marvelous event is miraculous, both because it is contrary to the constant laws of nature, and because it has not been produced by any natural cause. It seems to us that in order to demonstrate the first assertion, it is unnecessary to use a large number of words or great subtlety of reasoning, because it is established with ease by the simple basic qualities of the picture. Indeed, the entire picture, whether one considers the canvas or the composition of the colors of which it is formed, is nothing but an assemblage of dead, inert materials. And when one sees this dead and inert material form into an image which moves its pupils, raise them up to the point where they disappear beneath the eyelids, turn back and return to the normal state which the artist gave them, as if it were a living, breathing person, it becomes quite impossible to suggest that this is achieved by natural means or by the ordinary laws of nature. One is forced, on the contrary, to assert that it is the result of a supernatural and divine intervention. One can carry out whatever research one might wish, and produce all the arguments imaginable, and still will never succeed in persuading a reasonable person that this can be the effect of a natural law and some intrinsic quality of the picture.

As to the natural causes which could have produced it, if we leave on one side overexcitement and prejudice of the imagination, or the weariness and shakiness of the eyes when they have been fixed for too long a time on an object, or any other illusion which might be produced in the eyes of the observers; all which causes, apart from the fact that they do not exist, could never make an impact on the minds of intelligent witnesses who have been attentive and have been blessed with a good view which we cannot imagine could be capable of being destroyed. For, much as one might be able to invent causes, there are only two in our opinion which, on any sound basis, could damage the truth of the marvelous event. One might be a case of man-made deceit; the other might have its origin in the properties of light: but neither of them have any part in the event which we are considering. This is true, first of all, because not a single trace of human trickery has been detected, and that is also true of the properties of the light; experiments that have been carried out prove this with evidence. The proof that there has been no deception is clearly shown, not only by the fact that, of the thousands and millions of people who have studied the picture from very close up, not one has seen the slightest artifice which might explain the amazing movement of the pupils; but even more so by the depositions made concurrently by scientists, wise men and reliable experts who had been called officially by the ecclesiastical authorities to examine the picture. Indeed, Canon Tomasso Cerpesi (Archdeacon of the cathedral, professor of Physics and Mathematics in the venerable seminary), Count Ruggero Baldini (Doctor of Chemical Science), Girolamo Agnelli (Doctor of Medicine), and the two distinguished painters Luigi Pendrizzi and Niccolo Agostini, had met together in front of the holy picture on the evenings of May twenty-first and June first, and carefully examined it in the most minute detail. And having declared that the picture before them was the one known by the name of the Mother of Mercy, declared on oath that they did not find in the said picture any alteration or any unusual material, either in the canvas or in the holy image; any subsequent alteration in the color; or any removal or replacement in one or several parts of the picture; and that, in the space of eleven days that had elapsed between their first and second inspections (a noteworthy period, because during this interval of time, the marvel appeared almost continuously), they had not found the slightest trace of the least alteration.

Now, in order that we may conclude that no natural cause produced the marvel, it remains for us to speak about the effect of the light. In order to do that fully, we should examine its properties in detail, but since this would be an enormous subject, we will just say in a few words what is necessary for our subject, for the instruction of intelligent people.

That is why we suggest that, as far as it is given us to know, if the marvel is to be attributed to the natural effects of the light, one must have recourse to the following causes: First, to the **refraction** of light, whereby the rays, as they pass through the layers of air which is full of varying amounts of vapor (especially in church), could produce the phenomenon of displacement. Second, **reflection** of light at different angles, caused by the fluctuation of the flame of candles which, at the lowest angle and giving a larger amount of reflected light, or vice versa, can result in visibility which is more or less clear, more or less total or partial, of the white of the eye, which, in the case of a painted image, is most often far from uniform. Third, **diffraction** both by the interference of the light from candles symmetrically placed on the two sides of the image and, at the same time, the fluctuation of their flames, which might have produced varying levels of dark and luminous fringes[3] in the middle of the picture, but also could have made the fringes themselves flicker on the different parts of the eye. Fourth, the **sensitivity** of the eye which is more or less strong, more or less weak, depending on how long or short the action is which is undertaken by the eye, and how great or small the attention paid by it. Fifth, the different **contraction** of the muscles of the eye, which are capable of modifying the roundness of the sphere and the size of the pupil, so as to vary the amount of light supplied to the retina. Sixth, and finally, the involuntary, non-reasoning **movement** of the eye, which can result in a faulty judgment being made about the position of an object which is going in the opposite direction to that of the eye.

But all these supposed causes evaporate one by one in the face of the irrefutable testimony of the facts. Without here entering into a minute examination of the subject, which would require a treatise rather than a simple account, we return to the facts themselves, and once they have been appreciated, combined with the deductions of science, all people of intelligence will conclude that any cause which is supposed to depend on an illusion of the light is just imaginary, and they will reject such an idea completely.

Nevertheless, in order to further clarify the subject, we do think it useful, provided one is blessed with sound judgment, to explore here an argument which should demonstrate from this point that the marvelous event cannot be the result of an illusion. We might start by observing that natural effects, whatever they are, are invariably produced whenever the cause and the circumstances are

---

3. Light has the properties of a wave motion, and the light wave thus will have crests and troughs. If two beams of light join together with crests and troughs coinciding, the two beams will reinforce each other and an intensified image will result. Alternatively, if a crest of one coincides with the trough of another beam (i.e. they are out of synchronization,) the beams may cancel each other out, so that no image of the beams is seen. When light is passed through a very thin slit the light is refracted, so that beyond the slit an eye perceives multiple parallel images of the slit resulting from alternately reinforced and cancelled beams called 'fringes.' This is easily demonstrated when sunlight passes through a door barely ajar. Instead of a single vertical image or shadow of the light projected on a wall, one sees multiple parallel lines of dark and light as the light passing through the door gap is refracted and multiple fringes (parallel vertical shadow lines) results.

the same. If that is true, one would not be able to dispute it. But this is most certainly not the case in the present situation, for whilst, for many years, the holy image had been exposed to public veneration in the Church of Saint Clare, and in the same situation in which it was on May eleventh, when the marvelous movement of the sacred eyes was seen for the first time, no one in the past had ever noticed anything similar, and no one ever said that they had seen the marvel as it was seen on that day and by a large number of witnesses on the days that followed. In the second place, any natural effect which emanates from the play of rays of light should only be noticeable at certain points when the light is coming from the same side, because, if one changes the position of the observer or the direction of the light, the angles are no longer the same, and, as a result, the illusion either ceases completely, or will be produced at a different point. But one cannot even put this idea forward in the case of our marvelous event, because the movement of the holy pupils was observed in different places, from differing points, and in differing circumstances. It was seen in the chapel of Saint Clare, without lights; in the evening and in the morning; a little before midday; with and without the curtain on the window; and also after several candles had been lit in front of the image. It was seen when the image had been placed on the high altar and when it had its glass, but much more clearly once the glass had been removed. It was observed during the solemn procession, even though the circumstances and the natural causes were entirely different, and especially in the public square when the holy image was stopped so as to confer a blessing on the people. It was seen at Saint Augustine's over several months, even though, to comply with advice that was dictated by prudence, the holy image was sometimes placed higher up and sometimes lower; it was sometimes lit by one window, sometimes by another; or on occasion surrounded by several candles, sometimes placed below and sometimes above the picture, and sometimes completely removed to avoid the haze caused by their light. Despite these countless proofs and infinite precautions, the marvel could be observed at the same time by those who were in front of it as well as those at the side of the holy image, both when the church was full of people and when there were but a few present. We believe that we can state without fear, after all we have said, that the light could not have contributed anything at all to support the idea that our wonderful event was a natural effect from a natural cause. But if it is contrary to the constant laws of nature; if it could not have been produced by trickery or by the play or mix of light, we are compelled (as long as it is not suggested that it is the result of an act of the devil, which in the circumstances would be as ridiculous as it is insane) to conclude, with the most fervent conviction of our spirit, that it is miraculous and that it is the work of the almighty hand of God.

CHAPTER VI

*Sworn statements from witnesses of the marvel
on May eleventh and twelfth in the small chapel of Saint Clare's.*

It is clear and evident, by all we have said in the previous chapter, that the marvel has all the characteristics of a miraculous event. But is that enough? No, without doubt. It remains to be seen whether there are certain and indubitable proofs that establish the reality of the events, and that is the objective which we will examine from now on, and for which we will provide the proofs, so that the remainder of our proposition might be confirmed. As we have already said, we draw these proofs from the witness statements. We maintain that, in the context of the event under consideration, they are of the greatest value, both because they are provided by the most honorable people, under oath and in a holy place, but also because they were obtained by a formal legal process which was conducted and concluded with a level of care that was beyond reproach, and with all the safeguards that are prescribed by the holy Canons and by the decrees of the Council of Trent in connection with such an important and delicate matter. In this process (whose "exactitude" and "precision" were acknowledged by the Sacred Congregation of Rites, to which, for greater certainty, it was sent and submitted, and which it praised highly) there is recorded not only the movement of the holy pupils vertically and horizontally and a certain alteration in the holy face, but also the continuation of the miraculous event throughout the considerable space of almost eight months; with, however, the one difference that, in the first three months, the marvelous event was seen several times each day, but, during the last five months only on certain days.

From the quantity of depositions supplied during the judicial process it is clear that the number of witnesses was huge, and, one might almost say, equal to the number of people who visited the holy image. But the ecclesiastical authority restricted itself to recording only a certain number of them which was small by comparison with the total number that had been provided, but by the integrity of their faith, science, birth and social position they were more than sufficient to demonstrate the miraculous movement. We would like to reproduce all of them here, but as this work would become infinite, and require us to transcribe the voluminous process in its entirety, we will restrict ourselves to those which appear to us to be the most important, according to the approach we have adopted, and save an accurate list for the end. We might also just pause at this point to remark that the way in which the inquiry was conducted has resulted in the depositions being in such a form that they appear to belong to one single person. Let us proceed, and start with those people who saw the marvelous event in the small chapel of Saint Clare.

Apart from Countess Anna Baldini, who had the good fortune to notice the first of the supernatural events, and Eleanora, née Marchesa Buonadrata, as well as the four other women whom we mentioned in the second chapter, and who all clearly and with certainty (some on May eleventh and the others on May twelfth, and later again and at various times) saw the pupils of the holy image lift up to where they were hidden under the eyelids and then return to their usual place, and even move in a circular fashion; from among several other witnesses, we might mention in particular four priests and a layman who, on the same day and in the same small chapel, observed the marvelous events. Gaetano Nicolini, who had come towards the evening to find out for himself about the curious event, entered the chapel of Saint Clare along with a crowd of people. Going inside the small chapel, he positioned himself in a convenient position that was so close to the holy image that he could have touched it with his hand, and he affirmed that, to his great astonishment and with great excitement, he clearly saw the holy image lower its pupils and raise them. He went out and was not long in coming back. "I placed myself," he said, "in the gap, and with my elbow resting on the mensa of the small altar, I applied myself to observing the holy image with even greater attention, and I was again able to see the movement, but in a different way, because I could see neither rising nor lowering, but a horizontal movement of the same pupils, which was repeated several times, so I remained convinced that this was not any sort of illusion, but a movement which was true and real."[4]

Father Pietro Rommasini, director general of the boys' orphanage, when he heard about the rumors going from mouth to mouth around the city, and not believing what he was hearing repeated about the marvel, decided to go and verify the matter for himself, and with his own eyes, as he puts it. Having also come close to the holy picture, to a point where he could have easily touched it, he avers, without any fear of having being mistaken, and with the advantage of an excellent view, "that, within the space of the quarter of an hour or so that I stayed at the spot, I saw with astonishment and excitement, the eyes of this holy image move four or five times, in such a way that the pupils raised up to the point that they disappeared under the eyelids, and they then reappeared and returned to their normal position."[5] This surprising movement, which consisted of the lifting of the pupils and hiding them under the upper eyelids in such a way that nothing remained visible other than just the white of the eye, and then their returning to their natural place, was observed and averred in a sworn statement by Canon Camillo Gardini.[6] Father Marica Mathini also saw a horizontal movement in the right eye,[7] and Procope Signorini, a little before the Vicar removed the holy image to the high altar, having fixed his view on the left eye in particular, states, " I, in the space of scarcely three minutes, saw it move, sometimes to one side, sometimes to the other, and then lower itself in such a way that the black part took the place of the white, and then raise and return to the normal position in the picture."[8]

These witness statements, by people of a probity and faith which are incorruptible, should suffice on their own to validate the conclusion that our marvel is possessed with a quite incontestable certainty, in the light of the Scriptural and legal axiom *"in ore duorum vel trium stat omne verbum."*[9] But we do not wish to

---

4. Process, p. 6.
5. Process, pp. 89-90.
6. Process, p. 117.
7. Process, p. 67.
8. Process, p. 197.
9. "In the mouth of two or three witnesses shall every word stand" (II Cor. 8, 1).

content ourselves with these depositions, and will produce many more which will shed light on and confirm the miracle ever more, as will be seen in the following chapters.

CHAPTER VII
*Sworn statements from witnesses of the miracle
from May twelfth through the eighteenth at Saint Clare's high altar,
both before and after the holy image's glass removal.*

If, in the small chapel where it began, the celestial wonder showed itself in a way which was so obvious, it was no less amazing on the high altar, both before and after the glass of the picture had been removed. The Blessed Virgin remained there exposed to public veneration until five o'clock in the afternoon on May eighteenth, and during all that time she continued to move her sacred pupils in a way that became increasingly plain, in the morning, at midday and in the afternoon, in the evening and when it was fully night, even though the daylight was quite different from what it had been in the small chapel, and even though for several hours she still had her glass, which was then later removed. During these days of blessing, anyone who went to this small church became a witness to the touching spectacle of a crowd of admirers, who, each time the marvel was repeated, gave witness to it by the contrition of their hearts, the tears that came to their eyes and by the moving expression of the prayers or praises that they addressed to the powerful Mother Mary. Oh! How great God is! How extensive is his mercy! Oh, with what paternal care does He turn mercifully towards us! Oh, how in the midst of the corruption and distractions of an immoral and corrupt century He calls us to Himself!

And in order to confirm our words, we could produce a long list of the people who have solemnly sworn to have seen the marvel; but as that would require a great deal of effort, we will content ourselves with touching upon the judicial process, as it were, and only disclose a few pieces of evidence which will, however, be of such a quality that no one can fail to believe it.

The holy image had only just been placed on the high altar when Domenico Savini came into the church, went up to the altar, and with his eyes fixed on the eyes of the holy Virgin, he expected them to open and close, because he had been persuaded that this was the way the holy Virgin worked the marvel. But, as he could not detect anything like this, and, moreover, when he heard the people who were assembled in the church show by their actions and their words that they were seeing the miracle (as he himself could see nothing and he was not able to accept that the whole crowd was deluded) he began to think that God did not wish to favor him with such a great grace. But then, contrary to his expectations, and instead of opening and closing the eyelids, as he had been expecting, he saw, along with everyone else, the pupil of the right eye rise, disappear almost completely under the eyelid, and then return slowly to its former position. It was not just on that day that he saw this movement, but having come back the next morning at six o'clock, it was again granted to him to see the movement more distinctly in the left eye, and later, when the holy image had been stripped of its glass, he saw it in the two eyes, both day and night, both at Saint Clare's and at Saint Augustine's, and always from very close and in such a way that he could make out the most minute details of the miraculous face.[10]

To this evidence which acquires, in our view, a great authority because of the circumstances which accompany it, we can add another which is no less powerful; namely, that of Federico Lerini, notary and Guardian of the Public Archives of our city. Not having managed to find a way into the church on May twelfth because of the large crowd, he went there on the next morning at eight o'clock. When he got up to the step of the altar where the holy picture was, and having an excellent view, which meant he could be certain he was not seeing any illusion, he avers that during the time that he was there he saw the pupils of the holy image move horizontally two separate times, in the clearest and most indisputable way. On the next day and on the following days up to June fifteenth when he made his testimony under oath, he saw, as he attests, the same movement up to twice per day. He also declares that he saw a vertical movement and the holy pupils rise very clearly up to and under the eyelids, so that all that remained visible was the white of the eye alone.[11] This horizontal and vertical movement is also attested by Giuseppe Filippini,

---

10. Process, pp. 70-71.   11. Process, p. 85.

who saw it on May twelfth at eleven o'clock in the morning. and on two other occasions on the following days.[12] This is equally attested by the Director of the Pontifical Postal Service, Enrico Daddi, who observed it on one of the days we are speaking about, two hours before the *Angelus*.

We have another fine piece of evidence in the deposition of the famous portrait painter Cesare Sabattini. Having seen nothing before May eleventh, he was accustomed to visiting our holy image very often, drawn as he was by a special devotion to her, and also by the pleasure he experienced in contemplating this sacred face which, in his eyes, acquired a new beauty and new expression every day. Although he had looked at it with great care many thousands of times, he had never seen the slightest movement in its eyes. This was not the case, however, on May twelfth and the following day, while the picture was exposed on the high altar of Saint Clare's. Having approached the picture so that he could make out the smallest details, he clearly saw the pupils of the holy Virgin rise perceptibly, and in such a way that, for a few moments the white of the eye seemed more visible and extended, and moments later return to the natural state of the painting. As he had never seen anything like it on the numerous occasions that he had looked at the holy face, he believed that this marvelous event was true, all the more since it was confirmed by the witnesses of the crowd, who assured him that they had seen it at the same time; and also by the responses of the people who were near him and who, when questioned by him, replied that they had absolutely seen the same thing. All of this notwithstanding, he sought by using his hands to constrict his view to the face of the Virgin alone, so as to remove all possibility of an illusion, and so as to fully convince himself that it was not the result of a mistake produced either by the light of candles or by the light of day, or by his imagination. But even after taking such precautions he saw the same movements, not only at Saint Clare's but also at Saint Augustine's. Also, bearing in mind the experiences he had had and the excellence of his view, and knowing moreover that there is no type of skill in the painter's art that is capable of drawing pupils that can produce such perceptible and extraordinary effects, he

---

12. Process, p. 181.

concluded in his sworn deposition that he was firmly persuaded as to the certainty of a supernatural event.[13] This certainty is similarly confirmed by Dismas Venturini who, from May thirteenth through the seventeenth, from the footpace of the altar, saw the pupils of the Blessed Virgin rise and lower; and by young Gaetano Savini who declares that every time he went to Saint Clare's—and he went often—at different times of the day and night, both before and after the glass of the holy image had been removed, he was always fortunate enough to see the rising of the pupils of the Blessed Virgin, and especially that of the left eye, up to the point where they were hidden behind the eyelids.[14]

We could stop here, because the evidence produced, which can be read at length in the judicial process, and which is available to be read by anyone, appears to us to demonstrate clearly that the image of the Blessed Virgin turned and raised her pupils, by day and night, and with or without the glass, throughout the time that it stayed on the high altar of Saint Clare's; but we would also mention that thirty-six other persons, ecclesiastics as well as secular, also saw the marvelous event, and have affirmed it under oath.[15] To our great regret we must pass over them in silence, so as to avoid superfluous wordiness. However, we will not conclude this chapter without reporting the evidence of the four principal witnesses, who swear to have seen the marvel when the image was without its glass, and which is evidence we cannot leave aside without going back on what we promised to say. This evidence is that of Commander Audifax, the Marquis Diotavelli; that of Count Alessandro Baldini (doctor in both senses); of Canon Archpriest Michele Agulani; and of Archpriest Giovanni-Battista Mengozzi. All four of them saw the marvel in a way which excludes the slightest doubt. Indeed, the first of them testifies as follows: "I went to Saint Clare's and went up to the high altar close to the footpace, and having been there for around twenty minutes I saw at intervals, and on five or six occasions, that the image of the Most Holy Virgin, which was exposed on the high altar, moved its pupils horizontally and also vertically, to the point where they were almost completely hidden under the eyelids, and all of this

---

13. Process, pp. 130-131.
14. Process, p. 73.

15. Process, in various places, from pp. 61-285.

in a way which was so marked that I had no doubt at all about the reality of the marvel."[16] The second of the witnesses, who had a binocular of high quality that was perfectly focused on the sight, testifies: "I could perfectly make out the most minute details on the face of the holy image, and without any fear of being mistaken, I saw and remarked that the pupil of the left eye of the Blessed Virgin, towards which I was directing my observation, raised slowly and was then hidden under the eyelid, so that nothing remained visible but the white of the eye, and it then reappeared in the same manner. This action was then repeated three or four times in succession."[17] The third said: "On the evening of May fourteenth, at Saint Clare's, I saw with certainty, and very distinctly, the elevation of the pupils of the two eyes, up to the point where they were lost under the upper eyelids, and their lowering to their natural position in the picture."[18]

Finally, the last witness expresses himself as follows: "One day in the month of May at Saint Clare's, at eleven o'clock in the morning, while the image was without glass, I had approached the footpace of the high altar where the image of the Most Holy Virgin Mary was exposed, and I saw most clearly that this holy image moved its eyes and turned its pupils to the right and to the left on several consecutive occasions."[19]

This is why, we conclude, that if we are prepared, not only to believe in some event or other which is presented to us when it may be based on less solid proofs, but even to hold it as undeniable, how can we doubt this event when it is presented to us so clearly and it is so incontestably affirmed? Perhaps the people who testify to have seen it are not worthy of our faith in them? Perhaps they only saw it on one occasion, and with some element of uncertainty? Perhaps they are playing the game of betraying their own consciences by violating the sanctity of their own oaths? But no! Religious virtues, integrity of life, uprightness of intentions, the authority of doctrine, public esteem surround their names with such brightness that we have to have complete confidence in them and believe in their word.

16. Process, p. 92.
17. Process, p. 83.
18. Process, p. 158.
19. Process, p. 77.

CHAPTER VIII

Sworn statements from witnesses of the miracle at Saint Augustine's.

Wonderful as the miraculous image was at Saint Clare's, it was no less so at Saint Augustine's. The further one advances in the judicial process, the more the testimonies multiply, and, what is better, the more they acquire authority. Following our plan and as the next step in our reasoning, we will produce them successively so as to shed light more and more on the truth of the marvel. Although the proofs resemble each other greatly, and this risks a certain amount of uniformity in the content and form of our account, we are nevertheless not going to dispense with setting them out. We are convinced that people of sound judgment will easily excuse us, and we are firmly persuaded that religious and pious people will derive great pleasure from them, and will attach a great price on seeing increasingly confirmed the certainty of this miraculous event.

Our Blessed Virgin having been translated to Saint Augustine's and placed on an altar which, because it was in the middle of the church, received full light, continued to display the movements which we have already described. And, in order to establish the truth of them, we have here the most remarkable, and most unequivocal, evidence which lends to the events a new degree of certainty and reliability. Among the people who have, in this world, had an advance taste of the delights of this wholly celestial spectacle, we have, first of all, the most eminent Prince Cardinal Luigi Ciacchi; we have the Bishops of Pesaro, of Cesena, of Faenza, and Monsignor Milesi Pironi, the delegate of Urbino and Pesaro. All these important persons attest and swear under oath in their letters to our Bishop, to have seen, some on May seventeenth, others on the twenty-second; some on the twenty-third, others on the twenty-fifth, the miraculous movement of the pupils of the holy Mother of God.[20] We then find many others, whose evidence we give quite simply. Luigi Gucci, of Pesaro, came to Rimini on May twenty-first and went on his knees on the first step of the altar where the miraculous picture was, and he saw the pupils of the holy image, particularly that of the right eye, rise and disappear

---

20. Supporting documents nos. I, II, III, IV, V, & VI.

under the eyelid and then return to their normal place. He got up and moved to a better place, took a small binocular, and saw the same movement again, not only on this occasion but on every occasion when he returned to the church that same day.[21]

Count Francesco Bracci Vitelli, also from Pesaro, after explaining that on the evening of May twenty-fourth he had approached the holy image so as make out the most finely drawn parts, and that he had not been able to discern any movement, arriving as he did when there were numerous people there. He recounts that he came back the next morning at nine o'clock. and that he positioned himself in the same spot as on the previous evening. These are his own words: "I saw the eyes of this holy image, which I was observing with the naked eye, make a vertical movement downwards in such a way that the black part of the eyes, which had been partly hidden under each of the upper eyelids, became entirely visible, or, to put it better, appeared as a complete circle. In the lowering movement, I noted that the largest part of the white of these same eyes was quickly hidden; and after a very short pause there was a slow upwards movement, and as a result of this movement, part of the black area returned under the eyelids, so that the eyes returned to their normal state."

Count Annibale-Vincente Ranuzzi of Bologna came to Rimini on May twenty-sixth to see and venerate the holy image which was displaying the supernatural marvels. He expresses himself as follows: "I entered the Church of Saint Augustine, and knelt on the first step of the altar where the holy image was exposed on its own on the tabernacle. I had only just started looking at it when I immediately saw a noticeable lowering in the holy pupils which normally looked upwards; they turned down and then promptly went back to their normal position... I remained in front of the altar for around twenty minutes and in the most positive way, on three separate further occasions, I saw the same movement repeated in the eyes of the image, all of which filled me with excitement and spiritual consolation.[22] The evidence of Count Alessandro Turrini Rossi, who was with Count Ranuzzi and who also saw the same movement at the same time, agrees completely with this deposition.[23]

21. Process, pp. 256-257.
22. Process, p. 215. Supporting documents no. IX.
23. Process, p. 215. Supporting documents no. IX.

Her Excellency Margarita Montini, Princess of Santa Croce, on one morning at the end of May or the beginning of June, approached the image of the Most Holy Virgin Mary so that she could make out the smallest details of this sacred face, and she affirms that, on seven or eight occasions during the celebration of a Mass, she saw the rising movements so that the black part of the eyes sometimes disappeared completely under the upper eyelids, as well as the lowering movement. She also saw the horizontal movements from right to left, and left to right, and when the pupil rose, the lower eyelid also rose. She points out that all these movements were observed by her both before and after midday, and always alternately, and she did not observe the two eyes move at the same time.[24] Filippo Monaci of Fano also observed the surprising miracle on June twenty-seventh, and in his deposition which was made on the same day, says: "I went up to the footpace of the altar and fixed my eyes on the picture, but saw no movement in the eyes of the Most Holy Virgin; I was, however, surprised at the look of the face, which truly had about it something superhuman. Having come down because Mass was about to start, I knelt on the bottom step of the altar, and I raised my eyes to the picture. Then, without any shadow of the slightest doubt, I saw the pupil descend to the center of the eye, stop there for a moment, turn quickly to the left and then gently return to its normal place in the picture. I also noticed that at the same time the face took on a severe look, which filled me with a certain, albeit delicate, fright. I saw this movement at short intervals during the whole of the Mass until Communion, and I saw it repeated during another Mass."[25] Father Bernardino Celada, Rector of Saint Michael's, Ferrara, testifies that on several occasions on the days from July third through the fifth he observed the movement of the rising and lowering of the sacred pupils, sometimes slowly and sometimes quite quickly, and also horizontal movement in the left eye alone. Father Carlo Martignoni, also of Ferrara, and a doctor of Theology, asserts in his deposition that, on several occasions on the same days from July third through the fifth, he saw the pupils rise up to where they disappeared under the eyelids.[26] Canon

---

24. Process, pp. 323-324.
25. Process, p. 173.

26. Process, pp. 301, 302, & 304.

Sebastiano Perrelli of Ancona, who went to Rimini as quickly as he could to visit the marvelous image of the Most Holy Virgin, attests that on July eleventh he placed himself in front of the altar of the miraculous Virgin where he could observe it, and he was not able to detect the slightest movement in the eyes, but, when he came back to the same place an hour later, "Not only," he says, "did I see the pupil of the right eye rise to the point where it disappeared under the eyelid and then reappear, but, what is more, after a few moments I noticed that the two pupils turned horizontally in a most distinct and marked movement; and in the space of the twenty minutes or so that I remained in that place, I saw it repeated several times."[27]

We can add to these depositions the testimonies under oath of Canon and Doctor Antonio Cauzia, and of Father Giuseppe Pini, parish priest of Saint Gregory's, both from Bologna;[28] of Father Zefirino Gambetti, Canon of this Cathedral;[29] of Count Gaetano Battiglini;[30] of Father Giuseppe Scardavi, archpriest and vicar Moderator of Saint Paula's;[31] of Giacomo Grassi,[32] of Luigi Forchi,[33] as well as that of Domenico Savini, Dismas Venturini, Federico Lourini, and of Father Pietro Rommassini, whose statements we have already reported, and of fifty other witnesses. In other words, of seventeen ecclesiastics and thirty-seven lay persons,[34] and whose evidence, both from close up and far away; in calmness of spirit and without bias; on occasions repeated a hundred times; from different positions and at different times; in full daylight and at night; with the naked eye and with excellent binoculars, have asserted that they have appreciably, clearly and indubitably seen the reported movements, both horizontal and vertical,[35] and in such a way that it seemed to them that they were not looking at a painted, lifeless image, but at a truly living and animated person. If we examine all of these circumstances, we believe that we are able really to affirm, without any fear that we are mistaken, that there is no doubt about the certainty of this marvelous event, and that we can unhesitatingly proclaim it to be supernatural and miraculous.

27. Process, p. 207.
28. Supporting documentation VII, VIII.
29. Process, p. 79.
30. Process, p. 121.
31. Process, pp. 139-140.
32. Process, p. 195.
33. Process, p. 82.
34. Process, pp. 70, 71, 81, 85, & 90.
35. Process, various places from pp. 50-341.

CHAPTER IX

Sworn statements from simultaneous witnesses of the miracle, as well as of verbal or signal intercommunicators of its happening.

Among the numerous witness we have mentioned so far, and among all those who feature in the process, there are very few who, as a greater guarantee of the miracle, do not also mention the witness of the crowd of spectators who saw the miraculous movements at the same time, and who vouched for them in one unanimous and distinct voice: "Look! See how the image is moving her eyes! See how she raises them, how she is lowering them, how she turns them, etc." While Father Gaetano Nicolini was observing the miracle in the small chapel, he asserts that he heard other people seeing the same thing at the same time as he did;[36] Mario Mathini, also, at the moment when he noticed the movement in the right eye in the same chapel, heard those present repeat, "Look! Did you see it...? She moved her right eye."[37] Likewise, Canon Camillo Gardini and Pietro Romasini depose that at the very moment that they were marveling in the small chapel at the movement of these supernatural eyes, the movement was simultaneously being attested to in the following terms by the other witnesses who were present: "Look, look, etc..."[38] What happened in the case of these witnesses in the small chapel happened with others when the holy image had been placed on the high altar. Commander Audifax, the Marquis Diotavelli, said, "I noticed that other people saw at the same time as I did." Count Alessandro Baldini, having expressed that he saw and observed the marvelous action, adds, "I was left convinced of the movement, not only as the result of my own experience, but still more so by the witness of the other spectators who saw it at the same time as I did."[39] The same can be said of the very numerous witnesses who made the same observation, not only at Saint Clare's, but also at Saint Augustine's. To keep things short, we will produce just a few of them. Count Annibale-Vicente Ranuzzi expresses himself in the following way in the deposition we have already mentioned: "At the same moment, Count Alessandro Turrini, my father-in-law, who was with me, made a sign to me that he had also noticed the movement, and at the same time I heard the crowd all around me give very clear witness that it had seen the miraculous

---

36. Process, p. 61.
37. Process, p. 61.
38. Process, pp. 90-117.
39. Process, pp. 83-92.

movement, uttering exclamations of blessing and mercy."[40] Giuseppe Pini says, "My excitement grew even greater when I heard the people repeat the name of Mary, recognizing that they had also seen the miracle."[41] Father Francesco of Fano, a Franciscan of the convent of Montemaggio, having sworn that he, like the others, had seen the miracle, continues as follows: "I noticed that other people were seeing the movement of the eyes at the same time, because I heard them repeat at the same moment, 'See! See!' and they cried out with an emotion that was close to tears, 'Oh Mary! Oh Mary!'"[42] But, in our view, another fine proof that is worthy of being repeated is the one supplied by Giacomo Grassi, whom we have already referred to. One day he was in front of the holy image during benediction of the most Blessed Sacrament, at the moment of the singing of the *Tantum Ergo* when, having raised his eyes towards those of the Virgin, he saw, at that very same moment, the holy pupils move, and he asserts that this movement was also noticed by the small children who were near him, because they drew each other's attention to it by saying with simplicity: "Look! Look! She is moving!"[43]

This simultaneous sighting of the miracle by the crowd of faithful seems to us to be very strong evidence; first, because it took place precisely at the moment when the observers, whose depositions we have, also noticed the movement; in the second place, because people from all sides gave their witness and signs of seeing the miracle only when it actually happened. But what adds a new level to the conviction and persuasiveness is that it was not only those people who had come together who saw the supernatural movements at the same time and in the same way, but many others who showed either by their shouts or by a pre-arranged sign when the miracle was taking place. In the second chapter we have already seen that the women mentioned there, either on May eleventh or twelfth saw the same movements all at the same time, and we have just heard Count Ranuzzi tell us that the miracle was noticed by his father-in-law, the Count, at the very moment that he saw it. But from among the numerous witnesses who could affirm for us either the one circumstance or the other, we wish to speak of a few others. The Reverend Canon Doctor Antonio Cauzi tells us: "Two observers were

40. Process, p. 215, Supporting Documentation no. IX.
41. Supporting Documentation no. VIII.
42. Process, p. 133.
43. Process, p. 193.

with me; one was looking with the naked eye, the other with the help of a small telescope; as for me—I was using my usual binocular. We had only just fixed our look upon the miraculous image when we distinctly saw the movement of its eyes, and this was repeated several times during the space of around the three quarters of an hour that we were observing, and the impressions which we had, and which we were careful to verify with one another as we went along, were in perfect agreement as regards both the time and the manner of what we were experiencing.[44] Father Domenico Fontana, Canon of the Cathedral of Pesaro, after affirming in his sworn statement that he had distinctly seen the miraculous movement, continues as follows: "Canon Ortolani considerably increased my certainty when he assured me, both by his words and by touching me on the arm (something we did to each other when one of the movements described above was taking place) that he also was seeing them at the same instant that I was." And what Canon Fontana deposed here is equally deposed, for his part, by his fellow canon, Canon Ortolani.[45] Many other witnesses had a similar experience, and all of them have solemnly affirmed it in their depositions. Indeed, we find such an experience mentioned in the evidence of Camillo Gardini; in that of Luigi Gucci, there is agreement with that of Count Ortolani of whom we have just spoken, and that of Master Abbendangeri;[46] in another deposition of Annibale Andreotini there is agreement between his deposition and that of Gustavo Crescentini.[47] In all these depositions it is openly stated that they all saw the miracle at the same instant and in the same way; by reciprocally alerting one another at the same time, either by the touching of one another's arm or by speaking, they were able to verify to one another the movements which they had seen. We have another proof of the same sort, but established in a different way, and we should report it here. Count Antonio Marazzini agreed with three other people to hold hands and to squeeze three times if they noticed any movement in the eyes of the Most Holy Virgin. Here is his deposition: "We saw that this holy image moved her pupil in the right eye, lowering it and then raising it back to its normal position; and at the same time all four of us squeezed one another by the hand, as we had agreed."[48]

44. Supporting documentation no. VII.
45. Process, p. 118.
46. Process, pp. 256-257
47. Process, pp. 301-343.
48. Process, p. 112.

From all of this evidence it is clearly shown that it was not only the people who saw the marvelous movements at the same time as the witnesses whose depositions we have collected, but the witnesses themselves, united and in agreement, also saw them together, at the same time and in the same way. Therefore, it seems to us that we can only conclude that no influence of the light on the pupils of the miraculous image, nor any illusion in the eyes of the witnesses, had the slightest part in the event we are examining; and as a result, our proposition becomes increasingly evident and incontestable, that the miracle we are speaking about is more than certain.

CHAPTER X
Sworn statements from witnesses of the miracle:
a) according to the image's different positions and levels of light;
b) in the public square; c) on the very mensa of the altar.

What we have said about the simultaneous view of the witnesses is enough to dispel the slightest shadow of any illusion produced by light having played any part in causing our miracle. However, so as to demonstrate this truth even better, we will pause a little longer on this point and say a bit more about it. The ecclesiastical authority, as we have already observed, did everything it could to verify the miracle and to be absolutely sure about it. It was not content with lifting the glass of the holy image and giving it to experts to observe and examine, but it also had the image put in positions that were sometimes higher, sometimes lower; sometimes surrounded by a great number of candles, and other times by very few; at times with candles placed above or below, or at the sides; or even sometimes in front of the picture. All these precautions were dictated by wisdom and prudence, because if these marvelous movements had been the effect of some kind of combination of the light, by such means it would have been easy to discover the cause. But all these experiments only made the miracle even more outstanding, and for the witnesses they became a new and unanswerable argument that increasingly demonstrated its supernatural character. And, indeed, that most prudent and diligent observer, the Marquis Commander Audifax

Diotavelli, having stated that he had seen the miracle very clearly, gives the following proof that shows his complete certainty: "I have judged," he says, "that these movements in the pupils of the Most Holy Virgin are the result of a true miracle, and not in any way a human and artificial work, and still less an illusion of the eyes, because I have observed the movement of the pupils in varying positions and with both a greater and a lesser number of candles. When I closed and refocused my eyes on a number of occasions, when I opened them again and fixed them on the eyes of the Virgin, I at once saw the miracle once again, and in the same way."[49] Federico Leurini, who was one of the most assiduous and circumspect observers, expresses himself in this way: "When I saw these movements of the pupils of the Most Holy Virgin at Saint Clare's, it was sometimes with more, sometimes with fewer, candles around the holy image, sometimes by day and sometimes by night and by the light of a window which was opposite. At Saint Augustine's, although the holy image was displayed on a different sort of day, sometimes at a higher point and sometimes lower, sometimes with many candles and sometimes with only a few, such candles being at a greater or lesser distance, despite these changes of position and of the daytime conditions, I always saw the movements, and remain quite persuaded that the cause is neither artificial nor natural—still less an illusion of the eyes—but the result of a true miracle."[50]

We could include along with these three very solid pieces of evidence many more where there are to be found the same confessions, all set out with the same level of assurance of a most complete personal conviction and certainty. We could produce them here in their entirety, but will dispense with them so as to avoid unnecessary length, so we will rest content with just mentioning the depositions of Count Antonio Marazzani, Dismas Venturini, Pietro Romassini, Don Luigi Busignani, Giacomo Tacchi, Father Luigi of Rimini, OFM; Father Costante of Rimini, OSFCap; Father Vicente Pistoni, OM; Giuseppe Philippini and Giovanni of Golini. These depositions can be found in the documents of the original judicial process on pages 81, 88, 91, 95, 97, 199, 112, 113, 172 and 192.

---

49. Process, p. 93.   50. Process, pp. 85 & 87.

But the miracle was not just seen in these numerous and differing ways; it was also seen under absolutely different circumstances. When we start to reflect on our miracle, seeing in it at the same time the completely open hand of God's Providence, it seems to us that God Himself has taken care, in a manner of speaking, to ensure that it happens in a way by which any possible doubt is completely obliterated and annihilated in the face of the miracle itself. It was not only within the august majesty of the churches where the miraculous image was seen to move its sacred eyes, but even under the open sky in the full light of day; because it effected the movement during the solemn procession on May twenty-eighth in the main square, during the blessing on the people, and after the blessing during the procession. Indeed, Monsignor Vicente Reggiani, the prelate of His Holiness, asserts that he saw the eyelid of the left eye rise to the point at which the pupil completely disappeared, and the black of the right eye also disappear entirely; and this was not only at Saint Augustine's, but again in the Square whilst the people were being blessed with the holy image, to which he was standing very close.[51]

Canon Ortolani, after beginning by saying that he had seen the marvelous movements in the Church of Saint Augustine, continues as follows: "But especially in the afternoon, in the public square, after the Bishop of Faenza had blessed the large crowd of people with the holy image, I saw the Most Holy Virgin turn her eyes horizontally from right to left and from left to right, as if she wanted to cast her look over the whole crowd of devotees who crowded round to gaze at her."[52] Don Pietro Romassini is also certain that he saw the sacred eyelids move during the same procession, since in his deposition he expresses himself in the following way: "The sight of these movements was particularly remarkable during the procession that took place on May twenty-eighth, because, after I had left the orphans, I returned to the procession and I approached the holy image which I had the good fortune to carry with the other priests; keeping my eyes fixed on it, I saw very distinctly that, for the instant that it remained at rest, it moved its pupils and raised them on high."[53]

51. Process, p. 211.   52. Process, p. 243.   53. Process, p. 91.

Considering the precautions and the care taken by the ecclesiastical court, as well as the measures it adopted, it seems to us, as far as the light is concerned, that it is sufficiently clear that it had absolutely no part to play in our miracle. As to the theory that an illusion could have affected the eyes of the witnesses; this is demolished both by the fact that sworn witnesses simultaneously saw it, and also by their precise observations contained in the evidence which we have reported, and their attestations, which exclude it absolutely. We are going to give a little more proof so as better to highlight the invalidity of the theory. In all honesty, the possibility that such an illusion might be produced in the eyes of someone who is looking from far off at an object of small dimensions is something we must admit, especially if the observer does not have an excellent or a perfect view, but that this can also be the case where a person sees an object clearly and distinctly from close range, is something we can neither persuade ourselves, nor suppose, to be possible. Now, we have witnesses who have observed the miracle from very close range—so near, even, that they could not have been any nearer than to someone they were talking to in a close and familiar way. Without mentioning again those people we have spoken about earlier who saw the miracle in a place from which they could touch the picture with their hand, let us listen to the Bishop of Ferrara who, having gone up onto the mensa of the altar, tells us in words of great beauty and gravity: "I was right in front of the image, whose eyes could not have been further from mine than a palm's length, and in this position I looked with the sort of anxiety mixed with fear that religion produces in such solemn circumstances. About five minutes had gone by and I had not as yet been judged worthy to see any change in the holy pupils, even though the crowd of faithful was showing by expressions of the most pious devotion that it was the witness to such a change. I therefore addressed a fervent prayer to the holy Virgin, imploring her to kindly bestow upon me, for her greater glory and the consolation of my soul, the grace to see a single sign of her sovereign power; and at that very moment (I weep as I recall it) I saw the holy pupils shine with vivacity, whilst moving from left to right and vice versa; then the left pupil rose to the upper eyelid, to the point where it was entirely covered by it, and the white of the opaque sclera came to take its place."[54] Reverend Don Romuald

---

54. Process, pp. 363-364.

Rocatini, a Camadolese, having deposed that he saw the movement of the pupils from above the mensa of the altar at the same time as the Bishop of Pesaro, continues as follows: "I immediately left for Pesaro, and, once I had arrived in that town, instead of continuing on my route, I felt myself so strongly impelled to return to Rimini that I obeyed the compulsion and returned to that city on the same day. I went to Saint Augustine's and asked the archpriest to kindly permit me to observe the marvel again from above the mensa of the altar. Around two o'clock in the morning, as agreed, I went to the church and having gotten up onto the altar I saw the pupil of the right eye move in a horizontal direction, so clearly that when I saw this movement repeated I was seized by such strong emotion and trembling that, on getting down from the altar I fell down half-dead."[55] The canon penitentiary of Pesaro, Don Salvatore Ortolani, of whom we recently spoke, attests that he saw the pupil of the right eye rise on several occasions and return to its ordinary place, not only when he was at the footpace of the altar, but also when he was kneeling on the mensa of the altar, which he had mounted in order to wipe the holy image with a white handkerchief so as to verify whether there was really a tear on the left cheek, as the people gathered near to the altar believed.[56] Finally, Reverend Francesco of Fano, who had also climbed up onto the mensa of the altar at around twelve-thirty in the morning. in order to touch the holy image with a few objects, deposes as follows: "I saw in the most marked manner the vertical and horizontal movement of the pupils repeated in a way which a living person would absolutely have been able to do."[57]

If, therefore, the miracle was observed in positions and conditions of light that were so numerous and different, in the middle of the Square, in the full light of day, and from above the altar at a minute distance from the lovely face of the Virgin, we have the utmost confidence that anyone who sets out to consider the miracle in a spirit of impartiality and sincere religion cannot but be convinced of the true and real certainty of the miracle, and to acknowledge it, in the light of all these reports, to be a superhuman and divine work.

---

55. Supporting documentation no. IV.
56. Process, p. 244.
57. Process, p. 133.

CHAPTER XI

The indubitable certainty of the miracle achieved by a seven-person experiment.

We find a powerful confirmation of the supernatural event in a new experiment which was carried out on the miraculous image by seven persons, and which, in our opinion, is without parallel.

Our Blessed Virgin had been at Saint Augustine's for six months, and the number of foreign visitors had much reduced, so the ecclesiastical authority thought it should return her to Saint Clare's. And so she was again transferred from Saint Augustine's to Saint Clare's on November seventeenth with the same solemnity that had accompanied her translation on May eighteenth. The marvel, as we have already said, was no longer as frequent as in the first months, and it only happened from time to time. The devotion of the faithful was in no way diminished by this, and the Church of Saint Clare was full of admirers of the image of the Mother of God. There were moments in the day when the sacred space was too small for the number of faithful involved; and from time to time some devotees stayed in the church all night to pass these hours of tranquility in prayer before the Mother of Mercy, allowing their truly Christian hearts to open more easily to the sweet emotions of religion and to heavenly contemplations.

It was the night between December ninth and tenth, a night which was memorable for the miraculous event of the transportation of the Holy House of Nazareth, nowadays known as the House of Loreto, when Monsignors Marcus Mathini, Don Luigi Forlivesi, Gaetano Nicolini, Luigi Forchi, Pietro della Santa, Antonio Vanini and Giovanni Lanfanconi planned to pass the whole night in the church so as to express their personal devotion and to ask the Virgin to look favorably upon their prayers. So, once they had been locked into the church at around ten o'clock at night, the idea came to them to carry out a novel and remarkable experiment, with a view to ascertaining without any doubt that the sacred pupils did continue to effect the miraculous movement. This proof consisted in drawing a white thread over the kind pupils. After having consulted the superior of the Missionary Fathers and having obtained their agreement, Marcus Mathini got up onto the altar and with all his heart and strength he stretched the thread over the heavenly face and across the divine eyes. After attaching it with two sewing needles which he fixed between the frame and the canvas and stretching it so that it touched the picture, he made it skim the lower edge of the black area of the pupils of the most sweet eyes of the Blessed Virgin. By this method, the line of the thread left no space over the pupils, and to anyone standing in front of the picture it looked like an irregular triangular area of white spaces formed by the thread itself, the pupils and the eyelids of the holy image; so that any movement of the eyes, in any direction, would necessarily be visible in the most noticeable and certain way that could be wished.

This being done, the seven witnesses started to pray in front of the altar. At midnight they started to recite together a novena that had been printed in Naples in celebration of the miracle of the Blessed Virgin, and based on the words of the *Salve Regina*. As soon as the prayers started they noticed a certain movement, but when they arrived at the part which contained the words *illos tuos misericordes oculos ad nos converte*[58] the movement of the sacred eyes was not so much pronounced as positively remarkable. So, interrupting the novena immediately, they drew closer to the altar and looked at these remarkable pupils with the closest attention they could, and they saw that the movements continued. So as to assure themselves still further, they went up onto the altar in turn, and at a distance of just a few palms from the blessed face they observed two movements, both horizontal and vertical, and (without fear of any illusion or mistake), they saw that the two irregular triangles grew or diminished, now on one side, now on the other, depending on the movement of the pupils. When these pupils rose up, with the black area of the eye coming away from the thread, they left a white space in the middle, which, once they had lowered and taken up their normal position, was once again filled and covered up, and was no longer observable. But let us listen to their depositions. Pietro della Santa says (among other things): "Towards midnight, at the precise moment when we were reciting the verse *illos tuos misericordes oculos ad nos converte* according to a novena printed in Naples in honor of this great miracle, we noticed a rapid movement which was then repeated so noticeably that we interrupted the novena; we approached the altar and a few of us even went up onto the altar and saw even more clearly that the holy pupils were moving from right to left, covering the triangular area:

58. "Turn thine eyes of mercy towards us."
    (Word taken from the prayer, "Hail Holy Queen").

sometimes one side, sometimes the other, according to which one was moving horizontally, and we observed this several times. But this was not the only movement which we noticed; the holy Virgin also raised her pupils, detaching them from the thread, so that, when they rose and were hidden completely under the upper eyelids, between the pupils and the thread we could see a white space which was then filled by the black of the eyes when they returned to their normal position in the picture. I saw these movements both when I was near the altar, and when I was on the altar mensa, when the face of the holy image was no further away from me than a few palms. I must add, what is more, that after I had climbed down from the altar I saw a movement of these holy pupils which breathed such seriousness and indignation that I was left as one half-dead."[59] Luigi Forchi deposes similarly: "While we were reciting the novena in honor of the Most Holy Virgin Mary, as recently printed in Naples, we began to notice some movement. But when we arrived at the verse *illos tuos misericordes oculos ad nos converte,* we had hardly pronounced these words when we all saw, at the same time, marked movements. I noticed several times that the pupils of the two eyes moved to the right and to the left along the thread, so that the unequal triangle was covered up by the pupils, sometimes on one side and sometimes on the other, and then reappeared. I also saw that the pupil which was touching the thread became detached from it and was almost totally hidden under the upper eyelid, leaving above the thread a gap of such size that it was not possible to doubt that a movement had taken place—still more so when the white line of the thread, which had been visible, was once again covered up when the pupil returned to its normal place. I saw these movements both at the time I was near the altar and when I had gotten up onto the altar mensa. Then, when I had gotten down, and while Don Luigi Forlivesi was there, at the sight of a very noticeable movement, he burst out sobbing and cried out that we must take away the thread, because the miracle was more than evident. I saw the movement at the same time as he did, a horizontal movement, but of such a kind that it appeared to come from a person who was showing indignation, and the thought of this left me with an experience of deathly cold."[60] Giovanni Lanfranconi, after deposing that he had not seen the miracle at all when the others were seeing it because he

---

59. Process, pp. 410-413.

was behind all of them and could not see the eyes of the holy image, carries on as follows: "But when they had drawn back a bit and I had got up onto the altar in my turn, I very clearly saw the pupil of the left eye skim the thread, move away from it and rise to the point when it disappeared completely under the upper eyelid, leaving a white space visible above the thread, this space disappearing once the pupil had slowly descended and gone back to its normal position in the painting, so as to touch the thread."[61] Father Marcus Mathini, after saying how, in the presence of his companions, he placed and fixed the thread, and having recounted the interruption of the novena following the words *illos tuos misericordes oculos ad nos converte* because of the noticeable movements which they saw at that moment, continues his deposition as follows: "Along with the others I got up onto the mensa of the altar, and as I was then at a distance of only a few palms from the face of the holy image, and thanks to the light of the candles which were burning at the sides of the picture, I clearly saw that the small white area of the eye, which I was staring at fixedly, and which formed an irregular triangle composed of the thread, the pupil and the upper eyelid, grew larger and smaller by means of a horizontal movement; and as my companions noticed the same thing at the same time, I became more and more convinced of the truth of the miracle."[62] This horizontal movement and the progression of the virginal pupils, sometimes to the right and sometimes to the left, along the line formed by the thread, were also seen from above the altar mensa and are attested in the depositions of Luigi Forlivesi, Gaetano Nicolini and Antonio Vanini, who are all people whose testimony admits not the slightest shadow of suspicion.

We believe, in the light of all of this, that we are not far from the truth in saying that, even without the numerous and serious attestations which we have produced, and which give to the miracle the ultimate degree of certainty, what we have just produced concerning the experiment carried out by these seven witnesses would be sufficient on its own. In fact, when we consider the witnesses, we find in them no ground for suspicion; and when we examine the proof which they have presented, and the way in which the pupils of the Most Holy Virgin were observed and recorded, the possibility of illusion of any sort is removed, and it is not even feasible to imagine it. Even if the

60. Process, pp. 406-409.
61. Process, pp. 420-421.

62. Process, pp. 402-403.

witnesses have no knowledge of, or reputation in the physical sciences, then, without needing to consider the actual knowledge that some of them, in fact, do have, we are clear that profound and extensive knowledge of science is not required. When the question is reduced to a simple one concerning the movements in the eyes of a holy picture, any reasonable man (and even an ignorant one) is allowed to observe and infallibly conclude whether such movements do or do not exist, so long as he has a good view, and he is placed in a favorable spot to clearly observe them and reach an unassailable conviction.

CHAPTER XII

Sworn statements from witnesses of changes in the miraculous image: the face's color, tears from the eyes, and lip movement.

Now that we have set out the marvelous movement of the eyes of the Blessed Virgin and brought as proof evidence of such quantity and quality that they have become free from doubt, it is both relevant and useful to our objective for us to move on and also speak of other miraculous changes which were noticed in our holy image, and which we draw from the official record of the Canonical Process. Several witnesses, having deposed that they observed the miraculous movements of the holy pupils, also attest that they saw the sacred face become pale and then recover its colors and life; several say that they saw the mouth move, and, finally, others assert that they noticed tears fall from the sacred eyes of the Virgin and run down her cheeks, where they disappeared.

But so that all of this might be understood more clearly, here are their depositions in full. First of all, we find that Francesca Megani, having declared that she observed the miracle of the eyes of the Virgin in the small chapel of Saint Clare on May eleventh and twelfth, adds as follows: "In the same Virgin I saw a change in her color, which was repeated twice; she became pale when she lowered her eyes towards the ground, and quite red when she raised them towards heaven."[63] After her, Pietro della Santa, when talking of the time that the holy image was on the high altar in the Church of Saint Clare, says: "I noticed, on two different days that, while she was raising her pupils, her face became pale, and when turning her look to face the people she regained her red color."[64] Canon Sebastiano Perrelli of Ancona, having sworn that he saw the movement of the pupils, continues as follows: "I also noticed, without any fear of being mistaken, that this holy image changed color; I noticed that she became successively pale and then red, despite the light being the same."[65] Father Zefirino Gambetti, Canon of this cathedral, on speaking of the two visits he made to the Virgin on May twenty-eight and June twelfth, asserts that he saw on both days a change in the face of the holy image, noticing that it was becoming redder (that is, more inflamed) which is not normal in the picture.[66] Similarly, Father Francesco of Fano, a Franciscan, deposes: "I would add that, several times, I saw a change of color and a passing from vermillion and red to pale."[67] Eight other depositions are perfectly in accord with these five, and we find the same thing attested by the Marchesa Eleanora Buondrata Borghesi, by Archpriest Giovanni Battista Mengazzi, by Father Luigi of Rimini, OFM; by Archpriest Canon Michele Agusani, by Angelo Perilli, by Mistress Teresa Ficodi, by Giacomo Grassi, and by Don Carlo Martignoni of Ferrara, as well as by several others, as can be seen in the Judicial Process on pages 32, 77, 97, 159, 169, 195, 205 and elsewhere.

As to movements of the mouth; they have been observed principally by Don Luigi Mattrini, Master of the Episcopal Ceremonies and Professor of Liturgy at the venerable Seminary of Rimini, and by Father Costante of Rimini, OFMCap. The former declares in his deposition as follows: "I saw the face turn completely vermillion, the red rising up towards the eyes, and at the same time a certain movement of the sacred mouth, like someone who would like to cry but cannot, and that greatly moved me, because I absolutely saw it as a miracle."[68] The latter expresses himself as follows: "I saw that this holy image of Mary, which at that time was without its glass, opened its lips a little. Being afraid that I had been misled by this first impression, I fixed my look more attentively, but the movement only seemed to appear the more marked to me, as I saw the chin lower with the lower lip and then slowly return to its place."[69] But this witness observed not only the movement which we have just described; he also saw a tear run down from those immaculate eyes. At the end of his examination, he put it like this: "I confirm every-

63. Process, p. 49.
64. Process, pp. 189-190.
65. Process, p. 208.
66. Process, p. 79.
67. Process, p. 133.
68. Process, p. 64.

thing I have said, but I have one circumstance that I consider to be especially notable to add: and that is, having twice seen at Saint Augustine's, a tear flow from the right eye of the same image of the Most Holy Virgin Mary." The same thing was observed on three separate further occasions by his fellow priest, Father Odoardo of Fonli; he also attests having seen a tear descend from the right eye, and disappear halfway down the cheek,[70] as did also Pietro della Santa and Domenico Vanucci, who both depose this circumstance in their questioning session, and affirm it under oath.[71]

Such are the results of the Process, which establish not only the miraculous movement of the pupils of the venerable Mother of Mercy, but also the change in color that took place on the sacred face, and the tears that came from the miraculous eyes. We consider, and hold as certain, that these depositions are more than sufficient to be sure of the true and real certainty of the marvelous event, and to stamp upon it a miraculous character, which was the conclusion we had set out to show.

Should someone have placed himself in front of our marvelous image, and exercised every possible diligence, but, nevertheless, not been able to see this miracle in a way that convinced him, without going into the personal or local reasons which would most likely have been the cause, we would reply that none of that can in any way annul the truth of our miracle, and we can prove this by one reason and one example.

The reason is this: that not having seen the miracle does not invalidate the proof of the very numerous other witnesses who clearly did observe it, and who have attested to that under oath. The example is the conversion of the Apostle Saint Paul on the road to Damascus. It is a matter of faith that Our Lord Jesus Christ appeared to him in the middle of an immense light, reprimanded him and threw him to the ground. *Saul, Saul, quid me persequeris? ...Ego sum Jesus... Durum est tibi contra stimulum calcitrare.*"[72] Paul was not the only one who heard the Redeemer, but he alone saw Him; and what of those who were with him, what did they see? Nothing. And why not? ...Because the pride of human wisdom bows before the mysteries of God.

---

69. Process, p. 99.
70. Process, p. 147.
71. Process, pp. 176-189.

72. "Saul, Saul, why persecutest thou me? ...I am Jesus... It is hard for thee to kick against the goad" (Acts 26, 14-15).

CHAPTER XIII
Graces accorded to the faithful through the intercession of our Blessed Virgin.

In the same way that, by means of the holy image of His Most Holy Mother, God worked the miracle of which we have been speaking thus far and made it go on for such a long time, perhaps so that people from the furthest distances might be able to come and contemplate it, so by her intercession He has granted to her devotees numerous and marvelous favors. Whoever enters the small Church of Saint Clare and turns his gaze towards the walls of the chapel and the altar where the sacred image of the Mother of God is currently exposed for public veneration will find first of all hung around *ex voto* hearts and small pictures, whose inscriptions and paintings recall either healings obtained, or great dangers avoided, or other special favors granted. We would like to speak of these graces and marvels, still more so because the voice of the people unhesitatingly attributes them to the Most Holy Virgin; knowing, however, that the ecclesiastical authority, although busy and attentive to gather the authentic proofs juridically and with a wise prudence, has not yet issued any judgment on this delicate subject, we will not dwell on them. We will say a word about just one of these graces, and although we are only speaking after an official and canonical process has taken place, under the terms of the prescriptions of Pope Urban the Eighth of blessed memory, we do not intend to attribute to this event anything more than simple human faith, and we submit our words entirely to the venerated judgment of the Church.

Young Paolo Baroncelli of Borgo Durbecco in Faenza contracted rickets, along with a glandular obstruction. His malady was so serious that the slightest movement caused him grave distress, and he experienced pains in his spine and in his lower limbs that were so severe and so unbearable that he could not stand on his feet without the use of crutches and a person to support him. For months, Doctor Carlo Martini tried all kinds of medical assistance that might relieve the unfortunate patient, but seeing that every type of remedy was useless on account of the hopeless nature of the ailment, he deemed it right to cease all medication for a while, and see if time and nature might not achieve what had been vainly sought from science. That is what he did: but far from diminishing and taking a turn for the better, the illness continued to grow and get worse by the day; so much so that the poor young man was so weakened and reduced to a level of prostration that he lost all hope of getting better. Now, it happened that the Very Reverend Paolo Babbini, his cousin, and parish priest of Saint Michael's at Faenza, was driven by devotion to visit our marvelous and Blessed Virgin; he took with him a shirt of the unfortunate young man, had it blessed on the altar and touched against the holy image, in the pious confidence that, if the patient put it back on, he would obtain by the intercession of the Mother of Mercy what he had not been able to obtain from human science; as events proved, that is what happened. Back in Faenza he went to visit his unfortunate cousin at around two o'clock in the afternoon on June sixth, and he gave him the blessed shirt just at the moment when the illness had reached the greatest intensity possible. The patient took it with great fervor and, full of faith in the Most Holy Virgin, he put it on again. Oh, Marvel!...at once he felt himself delivered from all illness, and so strong and vigorous that he immediately began to run around freely and nimbly, and to go up and down the staircase of the house without any assistance, and without the need of crutches or the help of anyone else. Everyone present was filled with wonder, and his aunt was so affected by the sight of the marvelous event that she burst out sobbing, with tears of piety and consolation. But all the people who knew the young man, and who knew perfectly well of his illness were also surprised when they saw him come out of the house and go on his way alone and without any help to the house of the parish priest of Saint Anthony's, which was around a hundred paces distant.

Such is the event that happened in Faenza, in the person of young Baroncelli, a clearly marvelous event. It was recognized as such by the most excellent Doctor of Physics, Antonio Bosi, who was questioned on the subject by the public prosecutor of the ecclesiastical court,[73] sworn and affirmed on oath by young Baroncelli himself, by his cousin Father Paolo Barbini, by the Most Excellent Doctor Martini,[74] and by twelve other witnesses who, both before and after, deposed to the truth of this marvelous event; so that there was, as the jurists say, a general proof as well as a special proof of the instantaneous healing and of the perfect state of health of the young

---

73. Process, no. XIV.   74. Process, p. 3 no. V.

man up to the date of their questioning of him, which ended on August twenty-fourth.[75] If one reflects upon the nature of the illness which had been of the most serious and desperate kind, and upon the medical attestations of Doctors Martini and Bosi, such an instantaneous healing can only be attributed to a grace and a marvel through the intercession of our Most Holy Virgin, venerated under the title of the Mother of Mercy.

We think we should not pass over in silence another favor of our Blessed Virgin which is taken from a formal legal Process conducted because of it. This favor related to Master Leonardo, the son of Count Pietro Nardini of Bogliano. This young man had come to Rimini on June twenty-fifth with the population of the Vicariate of Bogliano to visit the marvelous Virgin and on returning, he got up into a cart, or carriage as it might be termed. Driving along with the rest of the devout company, he had almost arrived at his native town. A great number of the inhabitants of the village, who had stayed at home, learning that the procession, coming back from Rimini, was approaching, gathered together and went out to meet it. Alerted by the joyous sound of the bells and the displays of joy, the young man had but a single thought, to line up with the others, so as to arrive in the village with the same solemnity that had accompanied their departure. That is why, without taking care to stop his carriage (which was moving very fast) he jumped to the ground from it; but whether he did not take enough care, or whether the movement of the carriage was to blame, or whether his feet landed badly, the fact is that he fell backwards, and a wheel went over him at the point where his left thigh joined his body. Under the weight, which was heavy enough on its own, but which was further increased by the additional weight of the six or seven persons who were in the carriage, he felt as if his whole leg had broken and been torn off. He let out a piercing cry, and began to moan, as if he despaired of his life. At this sight and sound, the people from all around and other neighbors ran up immediately and lifted him from the ground, because he was unable to stand on his feet, and they placed him as comfortably as they could onto another carriage. In such a cruel situation, it is easier to imagine than to express with what fervor and piety he turned back to the Virgin to implore her help. The Virgin did not fail

---

75. Process, pp. 7, 8, 10, 11, 13, 15, 16, 17, 19 & 21.

to look upon him with favor, for, once they had arrived at his father's house, they immediately called for the surgeon of the area, Tomasso Benette, for him to give his professional assistance; despite examining the part over which the wheel had passed most attentively and as minutely as possible, to his great astonishment he was unable to find the slightest sign of damage or bruising, even though (as he also explains in his sworn deposition) a carriage of the kind involved, and loaded with such a weight, could not but leave some sort of damage in the part over which it had passed. Young Leonardo passed a fairly quiet night, and in the morning he felt so well that he got up, walked freely and boldly, and went walking around the village as if nothing had happened to him, attributing such a great favor to the Blessed Virgin, whom he had venerated in the morning. Once news of the event had spread, a miracle was claimed. The Most Reverend Vicar Forain, authorized by the episcopal court, commenced a judicial Process to examine the event, and from this Process it is established by the depositions of the young man, of the surgeon and of several other witnesses: that the wheel of the carriage passed over his thigh; that at the end of the accident he was unable to hold himself on his feet; that the doctor who examined him could not find the slightest trace of bruising; that on the next day he felt perfectly free and well, and, as a consequence, bearing in mind all the circumstances, this whole and complete preservation can only be attributed to a quite special grace of our Blessed Virgin.

CHAPTER XIV

Conviction of the truth and certainty of the miracles.
The growth of devotion to the Blessed Virgin.
Visits to the holy image. Its solemn coronation.

To what we have said about the movement of the pupils of our Blessed Virgin and the graces accorded by her to her servants, we think it would be useful to add the innermost conviction which took hold of our city, and which then extended out to the populations of the neighboring towns and then to places further afield. We base an important piece of evidence in the conviction of the large number people who were examined in the course of the legal Process, and who not merely deposed under oath that they had experienced a profound and unusual emotion at the sight of this marvelous event, but went on to explain the reasons for their absolute certainty.[76] We draw a further significant proof from the increasing attendance by the people at church and the Sacraments, and in the immediate ending of blasphemy,[77] as well as from the ineffable impact which the news of this amazing miracle had on the souls of the faithful, and even of non-Catholics: both in Italy, and all over Europe.

But it seems to us that a no less important proof is the immense gathering of the faithful, of every rank and gender, and the devotion to the holy image shown by them all. For several months on end the crowd of devotees was so large that the Churches of Saint Clare and Saint Augustine's were not large enough to accommodate them all, and such was the number of foreigners that Rimini itself often seemed too small to accommodate them, and none of this, in our view, would have been the case if they had not all been convinced of the truth of the miracle. But what can we say about the devotion which was awakened in souls towards the Most Merciful Mary, our Mother? We do not think we exaggerate when we say that there are no adequate expressions that enable us to explain it completely, or even to say what it was. In the presence of this blessed image there were to be seen only tears of contrition, exclamations of an ardent piety and faces absorbed in heavenly thoughts, inflamed by the most blazing emotion. All who came near the sacred altar of the beloved image were unable to pull themselves away from it, and could not have enough of the sight of this kind and heavenly face, whose beauty, it has to be said, is beyond compare, and which from time to time displayed the most attractive charms of such gracious forms that they exceeded all human imagination and earthly invention, and which it is only right to call divine. Furthermore, in the inexpressible transports which took hold of the devotees, so that they might have a lasting memory of the holy image and a sustenance for their piety, they had rings, chaplets, relics, clothing, medals, images and a thousand other objects of this kind blessed and touched to the holy picture: and from all quarters were published hymns, prayers and images of the Most Holy Virgin, in such large quantities that the lithographic and typographic presses of Rimini and other cities were not sufficient to satisfy the pious wishes of all the faithful.

76. Process, various places.   77. Process, *passim*.

But there was one solemn spectacle of special devotion, in the form of visits to the holy image by whole religious associations, by confraternities, societies and institutions of piety, and by large numbers of people who gathered together in solemn processions and giving external witness to the piety and religion in their hearts, drew tears of tenderness from those who witnessed them. It would be a great consolation for us to recall them all, with their holy and devout supplications, and even to describe them; but so as to keep things short, we will pass over many of them in silence, and confine ourselves to speaking of just a few of them, and even then not to go on at length, but to content ourselves with a quick sketch. We hope that this will not be the cause of reproach, and that we will be pardoned in good heart, because we are certain that the others would much prefer to see the honors which they have paid to the Virgin written up in Heaven rather than to find them recorded in our humble account. So, to begin with, from Feraro (as we have already mentioned) came in procession to visit the Virgin, first of all: His Excellency the Bishop, the Most Reverend Chapter and secular clergy, with part of the Confraternity of the city; then came the Most Illustrious Mayor, and then the parishes of Genestreso, delle Gabicce, Granarola, Castel di Mezzo, Saint Peter in Calibano, Saint Venera, Montecchio, Gradara, Holy Mary of Rebbrecce, Saint Bertold, Holy Mary of Monteluro, and della Romba. From Piano came the Friars Minor Observants, several ecclesiastics and the seminary students; the seminarians from Cesina came, and, from the diocese of Loggiano, the clergy and their famous and miraculous crucifix. From our city there went, with pomp and ceremony to visit the Most Holy Virgin, all the associations of piety, all the institutes, companies, confraternities and the archpresbyterial churches, and from the diocese a huge multitude of parishes, all of whom were distinguished by the number and piety of those attending, and principally from Savignano, Sogliano, Coriano, Montescendolo, Montefione, Roncofreddo, Misano, Saint Lawrence in Coreggiano, Saint Hermes, and Saint Vitus, seats of vicariates, accompanied by others of their dependent parishes, collegial churches, local authorities and magistratures.

The secular clergy of the city, especially the Most Reverend Bishop and his Most Reverend Chapter, although they had taken part in the two great processions with the holy image, wished to make a particular visit to the most miraculous Virgin, and so as to give this visit a special character, they resolved to carry out a solemn ceremony on the occasion; namely, to decorate the holy image with a golden crown. As it was not long until August fifteenth, a day on which the Catholic Church celebrates the Assumption of Mary into Heaven, they judged it suitable to carry out this task on that beautiful and memorable day. The Most Reverend Bishop therefore supplicated our lord, Pope Pius the Ninth, to grant the necessary faculties, and by way of response he received the following brief, of which this is a translation:

> *Venerable Brother, greetings and Apostolic blessings. Nothing is more in conformity with Our desires or is more agreeable to Us than to see grow more and more each day and spread in all places the devotion to, and cult of, the Most Holy Mother of God, the Immaculate Virgin Mary. This will make you understand, Venerable Brother, how great was Our consolation to receive your respectful letter of the nineteenth of the present month, from which We learn that you and the clergy of the city of Rimini are animated by such a lively desire to give the Most Holy Virgin a brilliant and public expression of your devotion and your gratitude, that you have already determined to adorn the image of the Virgin with a golden crown; which image, under the title of the Mother of Mercy, according to what you have told us, has, for more than two months, been famed for the marvelous movement of its eyes and is honored and venerated with great piety and devotion and an abundance of fruits for the faithful; and that you have arranged for this holy ceremony to take place on the fifteenth of the month of August next, a day each year on which the Church with pomp and solemnity honors the triumph of the Most Holy Mother of God raised to heaven.*
>
> *And, as you and the clergy of Rimini are supremely concerned to give this ceremony the greatest possible splendor, you urge Us, to this end, to grant you the authority to celebrate it in Our name and with Our authority. It is with joy that We hasten to respond to such a wish; there is nothing closer to Our heart or that could be dearer to Us than to do everything in Our power to turn to the glory and increase the praises of*

the Blessed Virgin Mary. That is why, Venerable Brother, We charge you by these presents, and with pleasure We give you the faculty in Our name and with Our Authority, to decorate with a golden crown this image of the Most Holy Virgin Mary that has the title of the Mother of Mercy; enjoining you, however, to observe everything which must be observed in such a ceremony; and further, should it be required for any reason, We also give you the faculty to subdelegate to whoever you wish, provided that it is an ecclesiastic of appropriate dignity, to the intent that such subdelegate may equally accomplish the same ceremony in Our name and with Our Authority.

What is more, with Our Apostolic Authority in the mercy of the Lord We grant to all the faithful of either gender who, either on the day of the aforementioned ceremony or on any day during the fifteen days that follow it, having confessed their sins and received Holy Communion, devoutly visit the church where the holy image is placed, and there fervently pray to the Lord for Our intentions and those of our Holy Mother the Church, a plenary indulgence and the remission of all their sins, which grace can also be applied by suffrage for the souls in purgatory.

With pleasure we also take the opportunity to send to you our warmest good wishes in the form of an apostolic blessing which we send to you personally with all our heart, Venerable Brother, and to the flock entrusted to your care.

Given in Rome, at the Holy See, July 25, 1850, the fifth year of Our Pontificate.

PIUS IX, Pope

When August fifteenth arrived, the whole clergy met in the morning at the cathedral and went in procession to the Bishop's Palace to meet him and they then began the processional walk towards the Church of Saint Augustine in the middle of a large crowd of spectators who had rushed up to gaze at the solemn ceremony which was about to be performed. This vast church was full of people of every rank. The holy image had already been moved to the high altar, and everything was in place for the festival. Once the procession arrived everyone took up the place which had been allocated to him. The Bishop and the Canons of Rimini went to a separate chapel where they solemnly recited *Terce*. His Excellency, having revested in his pontifical vestments, then went in procession with the Canons, the beneficed clergy and the seminary to the high altar in order to celebrate a Solemn Mass sung to the harmonies of specially chosen music. When the Mass was over, His Excellency, seated on his throne, addressed the people with a homily that was especially grave and touching, similar to the holy ceremony, concerning the amazing miracle and the need which all men have of the help and protection of the powerful Mother of God. He then approached the high altar and lifted the golden crown, which (in accordance with the prescribed rite) he placed on the head of the holy image whilst, with a sweet harmony, the musicians sang the verse *Corona, aurea,* etc.[78] Once this rite was over, they intoned the *Te Deum,* accompanied by the whole people, and thus ended the sacred ceremony. What beauty and what majesty! And what emotion it awoke in the hearts of the faithful, it is impossible to express, and only those who assisted at the ceremony and experienced for themselves are able to understand the sweetness and wonderful effects.

CHAPTER XV

Offerings made to the Most Holy Virgin.

The sentiments of devotion and piety towards the glorious Mother of God drew to Rimini a great gathering of foreigners and large numbers of people to venerate our miraculous image, and they also brought with them great quantities of offerings as proof

---

78. This verse is taken from a responsory sung during Matins for a Bishop and Martyr. Giovanni Pierluigi da Palestrina composed a motet for five voices using these words, which may have been sung on this ocassion.

R. Corona aurea super caput ejus, expressa signo sanctitatis, gloria honoris, et opus fortitudinis.
V. Quoniam praevenisti eum in benedictionibus dulcedinis, posuisti in capite ejus coronam de lapide pretioso.
R. Expressa signo sanctitatis, gloria honoris, et opus fortitudinis.

R. A crown of gold upon his head, wherein is engraved Holiness, an ornament of honour, a costly work.
V. For Thou hast prevented him with the blessings of sweetness, Thou hast set a crown of precious stones upon his head.
R. Wherein is engraved Holiness, an ornament of honour, a costly work.

of these sentiments. Of all those who went to visit her, we do not believe that there was a single one who did not leave behind the thing that was most precious to him, and these gifts came from those who visited Rimini and also from those who were unable to come. We will say something about these presents and about the pious faithful who offered them, but not everything, because to speak of each one in particular would require infinitely long passages, and impose on us an impossible task.

But let us begin. For the adorning of the holy picture, Cardinal G. Antonelli, pro-Secretary of State of our lord Pope, Pius the Ninth, sent a silver frame of exquisite design and workmanship, with gold ornamentation enriched with one hundred sixty-four precious stones, among which there were several of remarkable size, especially on the four corners and in the center. Count da Trapani, brother of the King of the Two Sicilies, sent a silver lamp which was very rich and elegantly worked. The Grand Duchess, widow of Grand Duke Ferdinand the Third of Tuscany, came in the company of His Imperial and Royal Highness Augustus Ferdinand and several people of his court to visit the Most Holy Virgin, and when they left they gave a precious gift of a gold collar on which were to be seen sixteen large rubies, thirty-two smaller ones, and three hundred twenty-four brilliants of different sizes. The Countess Maria Maddalena Verano Vicenti Mareri of Riuli sent to the holy image a veil of white silk embroidered in gold of an astonishing delicacy of design and workmanship, enriched with precious stones—a present which, in its richness and execution is in perfect harmony with the frame for which it is intended. The Dominicans of Mondovi gave a most elegant trimming of the finest thread for an altar cloth. Geatano Bedini, Extraordinary Commissioner of the four diplomatic legations and Monsignor Giuseppe Milesi Pironi, delegate of the Province of Pesaro and Urbino, each donated a rich silver chalice of fine workmanship. The Bishop of Pesaro gave a rich and fine monstrance; his Most Reverend Chapter, an elegant silver chalice; the most illustrious mayor offered from his own hands a most fine chalice and six table chandeliers in silver; the parish priest of the town, a silver ciborium; the College of Charity, a beautiful silver crucifix; and all the Confraternities gave either wax or silver *ex-votos*; the parishes of the diocese of Pesaro, called Holy Mary of Scabbrecce, Saint Bertold and Saint Marina gave two large hearts and a very fine silver reliquary; those of Monteluro and della Romba, also two large hearts and a silver reliquary; the inhabitants of Longiano: a rich silver chalice, and the magistrates of the same town, two crystal cruets embossed with silver with a tray and a silver bell.

But though all these foreigners showed themselves to be aflame with love for the powerful Mother of God, and made her such generous gifts and precious offerings, the inhabitants of Rimini were not to be beaten; the Right Reverend Bishop, the Most Reverend Chapter, the clergy and the episcopal seminary gave to the Most Holy Virgin the rich gold crown which decorated the holy image on August fifteenth, as we have said; a chasuble in gold cloth; an elegant missal and a very fine candlestick; and the seminary students also offered a frame containing a large number of silver medals which had been awarded to them a few days before, and which they had worn on their chests as evidence of, and reward for, their work and study of the sciences. The village of Montefiore with the parishes of the commune gave a silver censer and boat; the parishes of Monte-Tauro, Saint Patrick, Mulazzano, Caserolo and Vecciano, another silver censer and boat; the urban parish of Saint Agnes, a silver crucifix, six gilded chandeliers, the cloth and lace for three albs, four metal chandeliers, four porcelain vases and two bells. The suburban parish of Saint Nicholas, two silver lamps; the other parish of Saint Julian, a set of vestments in one piece, very fine altar linen, two crystal cruets with arabesques in gold, a heart and a name of Mary in silver. The Vicariate of Roncofreddo gave in homage two cruets with a tray and silver bell, and an amount of silver money; the Society of Town Servants, a bowl for holy water and a silver aspergillum; the region of Saviguano sent a damask cope decorated with gold braid, a chasuble in cloth of gold, an alb and an amice in very fine cloth; the Pious Union of Saint Cajetan, an altar frontal in silk with the name of Mary embroidered in gold, a cross and six gold plated chandeliers; the urban parish of Saint Bartholomew and Mariano, a very fine ciborium cover, embroidered in gold, and six gold plated chandeliers; the other parish of Saint Martin, a piece of white silk fabric for a cope, a chasuble of finely embroidered fabric and an alb decorated with very fine lace; the Corps of Engineers, Experts and Masons, an altar carpet; the Conservatory of Vulnerable Girls, a chasuble in brocade, three fine altar cards and a table of indulgences; the Vicariate of Saint Vitus gave a large quantity of wax and a beautiful silver medal with a commemorative engraving of the miracle and of their visit; the village of Verucchio gave a silver chalice which was equally remarkable for its design and for its workmanship; the public gymnasium of the commune and the Institute for poor children each gave a silver medal. All the other parishes, confraternities and pious unions gave either wax in abundance, or silver; and from among this number we must not omit to mention those of Saint Hermes, which, as well as other presents, offered a fine picture containing the name of Mary artistically made up out of silver coin.

As well as the gifts we have just described there were many more, consisting of around two thousand pounds of wax, and rings, bracelets, sashes, strings of pearls, coral, watches, collars, earrings, gold chains, crosses, medallions, crucifixes, hearts, chaplets and a gold rose; all in all coming to a value of around two thousand ecus[79], with more in silver placed on the mensa of the altar or left indiscriminately all around, or sent in from outside, coming to a sum of just about four thousand, five hundred ecus. The ecclesiastical authority and the commission set up for the purpose is using this sum for the enlargement, or rather the rebuilding, of the Church of the Most Holy Virgin, and the works are going on without a break; so, thanks to the piety of the faithful, we hope that they will soon be completed.

CHAPTER XVI

Conclusion and the Decree of the Bishop concerning the miracle.

From all that we have said so far, in a style which is not just simple, but perhaps even slovenly and not very meticulous, it is at least possible to deduce in a reasonably positive way, if we are not mistaken, as follows: that before May eleventh, eighteen hundred and fifty, no movement of the pupils of the sacred im-

---

79. The *écu* disappeared during the French Revolution, but the five-franc silver coins minted throughout the nineteenth century were but the continuation of the old écus, and were often still called "écu" by French people. If a single French Franc was worth about sixteen American dollars in 1850, which is a conservative estimate, then this amount would be equivalent to one hundred sixty thousand dollars in 2012.

age of our Mother of Mercy, or any other change in her sacred image, was seen; that it contained no matter capable of producing any sort of displacement and then return of any one or more parts of the sacred painting, or any changes in its color; that the holy pupils moved in four different ways (namely, from down to up and from up to down, and then from right to left and from left to right); that these movements were seen and observed, not just once, but several times in the day without interruption for almost three months, and a little less frequently for around a further five months; that they were seen and verified, not only in one single place, but in four quite different ones (namely, in the small chapel and on the high altar in the Church of Saint Clare; on the public square, and in the Church of Saint Augustine); that they were consistently seen while the holy image had its glass and after the glass had been removed, at daytime as well as night; with several candles as well as with no light; by people who were simultaneously gathered, be it in front of the picture or at the side of it; when the picture was placed in different positions (namely, sometimes low down, sometimes high up, sometimes at the side); that several people saw them all at the same time and in the same way, both from far away and from near at hand, both with the aid of excellent glasses and with the naked eye; both from above the altar mensa and at just a few palms' distance from the holy image; that when a thread had been placed so as to skim the lower parts of the pupils it was possible to discern in a most marked and clear fashion the horizontal and vertical movement; that this blessed face paled and recovered its color and a few tears flowed from the sacred eyes and disappeared on the cheeks; and that the heavenly lips moved. In conclusion, that a profound conviction in the truth of this miracle took hold of all classes of people and whole populations in an extraordinary way. That is why his Lordship, our Bishop, having examined at length and with prudence and maturity all the documents of the Legal Process; having consulted the opinion and judgment of serious theologians and wise and eminent men; having appealed to God for His aid and for the assistance of supernatural light in such a delicate affair of such great importance, finally pronounced the following signed decree, by which he confirmed the undoubted certainty of the miracle:

DECREE

We, Salvatore Leziroli, Bishop of Rimini, wishing to give satisfaction in the legal proceedings instigated by Signor Carlo Gaspard Venturini, Procurator Fiscal, at the request of our Deputy Chancellor, as well as to the devotion of the faithful, hereby state and declare that we have attentively read the depositions made under oath by the witnesses in the documents which have been drawn up; that we have carefully examined the evidence, and having consulted several theologians and a number of other pious priests, in conformity with the prescriptions of the holy Council of Trent (sess. **25, de invoc. sanct.***); after having invoked the light of the Holy Ghost for several days, and having seen and examined everything, we have decreed, and hereby do decree, that the truth of the marvelous movement of the pupils in the holy image of the Blessed Virgin Mary, under the title of the Mother of Mercy (which for a long time has been venerated in the Church of Saint Clare of this city, which was later transported to the much larger parish Church of Saint John the Evangelist and was finally returned to the said Church of Saint Clare), has been and remains proven, and we hereby permit and allow that the account of this great event, along with this present decree, be published, not only in the preceding manner, but in all other ways that may be judged better for the greater glory of God, and so as to rekindle in the faithful and ever more to increase their devotion to the Blessed Mother of God.*

Given at Rimini, in our Episcopal Residence, Saturday, January 11, Anno Domini 1851.

SALVATORE, Bishop of Rimini

This decree and episcopal sanction which authorize and confirm the truth of our miracle in such resounding terms, and which imprint upon it the seal of the most evident certainty, seem to us to be unchallengeable. And, in our opinion, they must triumph over any kind of opposition. The Church, in dealing with all the questions which appertain to her, and in particular with regard to questions concerning her nature, is full of foresight; she proceeds with a rare prudence, and her severity is far above that of the lay world. The slightest doubt is, for her, a reason for rejection, and she does not rest and is not satisfied until she has discovered the pure and real truth. Furthermore, leaving on one side several examples which could be provided of this, by way of illustration of the point we are making we would like to show the authority and weight of an Episcopal decree by reference to an event that has occurred recently in France. We do not believe there is anyone who has not heard of the event which is said to have taken place concerning the crucifix venerated in the Church of the Calvary of Saint Saturnin-en-Apt, Vaucluse, which is said to have drops of living blood running from its wounds. The secular authorities went to the scene of the event and, having carried out a careful examination, they confirmed their certainty, both by oral process and by authenticated letters, that the prodigy was true and real, and that they, along with many others, had been eyewitnesses; so that, once the account had been communicated by them to those in charge of the public press, the marvelous event was published by the newspapers of Avignon and Paris, and reported by many others in the Italian press, and it seemed to that nothing more was required for it to be accepted as beyond doubt. But the Archbishop of Avignon had the matter carefully examined by a commission which he instituted for the express purpose, and on the January twenty-fourth of the present year, eighteen hundred and fifty-one, he signed the report of the commission, which concludes that, after mature and careful examination, the supposed flow of blood from the image of the crucifix of Saint Saturnin should not be attributed to a true miracle.

We are coming at last to the end of our discourse and account. There is no doubt that this task was greatly beyond our powers; we have, nevertheless, carried it out willingly so as to satisfy the request of him, who, with the authority to require it, gave us the responsibility of accomplishing it. And, dear reader, if you have followed us up to this point, and if you have found in our account neither the strength of spirit nor the grace of language which the subject might have required, be indulgent and pardon us for not having been able to give what is not in us. As a stranger to all other thoughts, and holding in horror any other intention, our sole aim has been to make the truth and certainty of the miracle be known, whilst ignoring all the techniques of art, and we hope that we have achieved this, at least so far as it was incumbent upon us. If we have accomplished our intentions, we admit to you in all sincerity of our soul, that we have, and will have in the future, great consolation from the fact, because we have within our sight nothing other than the glory of God, the honor of the Most Holy Virgin, and the spiritual well-being of souls, at a time when the corruption of morals, licentiousness, incredulity and the war against religion have reached a point that cannot be surpassed.

Nothing remains for us than to wish, first of all, that, in the miracle which we have explained, the whole world might recognize the invitation which God is making to us to bring ourselves back and return to Him, and that we might then turn to the Most Holy Virgin and sweetest Mother of Mercy, to beseech her fervently to stoop down and cast her kindly look upon all corners of the earth, so that her look is one of succor to the faithful that enables them to march with greater certainty along the road that leads to heaven; a look of light for the blind who cannot see the rays of faith; of grace and rest for the lost, that they might return to the bosom of God; that with the whole world established in the calm of a perfect peace, the Catholic Church might reign sole and triumphant; that there might be just one single Pastor and one single flock, as was established by Our Lord Jesus Christ in Peter and on the corner stone upon which he placed the indestructible foundations of the Catholic, Apostolic and Roman Church.†

Editor's Note: The following appendices have not been translated from the original text and do not appear here.

- **Supporting documentation**
- **List of witnesses heard during the Judicial Process**
- **Table of sums offered to the Blessed Virgin and the way they have been used**

A PRAYER TO OUR LADY, THE MOST HOLY MOTHER OF MERCY

Hail, O Mother, Glory of Glories,
Queen of Heaven and Earth,
Sovereign Lady of the Angels and of the Saints,
Joy of the Just, and Advocate of Sinners.

Hail, O Beautiful Iris of Peace,
who always assists at the Throne of God,
So as to mitigate His severe judgments
against us miserable sinners.

Hail, O Mother of Mercy,
Immaculate Mother of God and our Mother,
Health of the Sick, Consoler of the Afflicted,
Refuge of those who have gone astray,

Hail, Queen, Mother of Mercy
O Queen, O Mother, do not reject from thy sight
thy miserable servants,
Thy faithful Sons who implore thy help
and depend on thy tireless munificence
And on thy maternal heart.

May thou bind our wounds
and obtain for us the pardon of our sins,
Restore the peace which we have lost,
Console us in our afflictions, help us in our exile,
And from the bosom of thy mercy hear our prayers
As we ceaselessly repeat
"Hail Holy Queen, Mother of Mercy,
Hail our Life, our Sweetness and our Hope,
Hail!

ST. JOHN BOSCO
the universal friend of the nation's children
on May 12, 1882
the 32ND anniversary of the first miracle
at this altar in celebration
offered the Holy Mass
and implored the help of the merciful Help of Christians
The Salesian alumni of Rimini
so that the memory does not wane
erected [this plaque] as a perpetual memorial in 1938

Plaque commemorating the attendance of Saint John Bosco at the thirty-second anniversary celebration of the miracle with the translation of the words below it.

Exterior of Church of St. Clare

Interior of St. Clare's with miraculous image over altar

Town Hall and Vittorio Emanuele Theater of Cavour Square

Church of St. Augustine

www.ingramcontent.com/pod-product-compliance
Lightning Source LLC
Chambersburg PA
CBHW031301290426
44109CB00012B/677